PRAISE FOR H

Healing Marks is truly inspirational, timely, insightful, and wise. Epperly shares his breadth and depth of knowledge in deft and accessible ways. He invites us to broaden our understanding and experience of spirituality by bringing together faith, health, body, mind, in ways that are relevant for everyday living as well as tackling the big questions of life. Through the lens of the Gospel of Mark, Epperly pushes beyond false divisions between mystical faith and rational thought and guides us into a greater knowledge, experience, and practice of hope, healing, and wholeness. This honest and challenging book engages hard questions rather than offering up disruptive theological platitudes or pathways of avoidance. *Healing Marks* is deep, profound, and useful. Individuals and groups will be rejuvenated by the experience.

Edwin David Aponte
Vice President for Academic Affairs
Dean of the Faculty and Professor Christianity and Culture
Christian Theological Seminary

"It has been said that theology begins where the pain is . . ." Hand in hand with the healing stories in the Gospel of Mark, Bruce Epperly begins where the pain is, and ushers us into the heart of the big questions surrounding illness and pain. Is the disease our fault? Is it God's will? Are we powerless in our pain? What role does faith play? Most theologians who try to deal with these difficult questions leave only more questions. We need an adequate theology that can embrace our pain without feelings of guilt on the one hand, or feelings of powerlessness on the other. No theologian I know deals with the difficult questions of faith and illness with more clarity and insight than Bruce Epperly. The healing stories of Mark suddenly become our stories, bringing us into contact with a new way of understanding what healing really means, one which brings about both emotional well-being and spiritual liberation.

Dr. Epperly deftly challenges the Calvinistic notion of an all-controlling God--popularized today in the writings of Rick Warren--in favor of a relational God of love and creative transformation. He sees Jesus as one who desires our active participation in the healing process. "We are not all-powerful, nor can we create our own realities," says Epperly, "but our decisions shape how we experience life and can lead to liberating hope and equanimity in the most challenging situations." Epperly does not just "theologize" from the ivory tower; his own personal experience with his son's cancer allows him an intimate look at pain from the inside. Epperly writes as one who understands; he also writes with a holistic view, offering us healing practices or "healing marks" to help unleash the healing power within. As a Reiki master teacher and one of the finest process theologians of his generation, he possesses the unique gift of uniting biblical text and theology with holistic healing practices, and doing so in an accessible, clear writing style. *Healing Marks* is an important book for those suffering illness, for pastors, and for all who love the stories of Jesus.

Patricia Adams Farmer
author of *The Metaphor Maker* and *Embracing a Beautiful God*

Without skirting hard questions and with extraordinary insight, Bruce Epperly shows how healing texts of scripture connect with the contexts and broken texts of ordinary people's stories to create transforming spiritual experiences. Healing, he demonstrates, is multifaceted in the Gospels and now: Jesus's touching dirt-poor sick folks and well-heeled tax collectors bids us to spiritual practices and social justice using scientific tools.

Kent Ira Groff
Denver, Colorado
Retreat leader, spiritual guide, and author of *Honest to God Prayer* and *Clergy Table Talk*

HEALING MARKS:

HEALING AND SPIRITUALITY IN MARK'S GOSPEL

BRUCE G. EPPERLY

Energion Publications
Gonzalez, FL
October, 2012

Cover Design: Henry Neufeld
Cover Art: © Loveliestdreams | Dreamstime.com

ISBN10: 1-938434-13-7
ISBN13: 978-1-938434-13-6
Library of Congress Control Number: 2012951594

TABLE OF CONTENTS

A WORD OF THANKSGIVING

This is a very personal book. It emerges from nearly thirty years of living with the healing stories of Jesus. I discovered these stories in a life-changing way as a young college professor, seeking to make sense of the growing interest in complementary and alternative medicine. My interest in personal and global healing increased during seventeen years as a chaplain and professor at Georgetown University School of Medicine, where I was among the first persons to teach courses on spirituality and medicine at a major medical school. Over the years, I have embraced Jesus' healing ministry as a pastor, professor, reiki teacher, and spiritual guide. I have wrestled with the meaning of Jesus' healing ministry and God's role in healing and sickness the hard way as a pastor, friend, child, spouse, and parent – with fear and trembling in hospital rooms, hospices, gravesides, and healing services. I have heard testimonies about the power of God to cure illness, but I have also sat at the bedside of dying friends and congregants, who have done everything right, according to the principles of their faith traditions and philosophies – personal and intercessory prayers, positive thinking and affirmations, meditation and diet, complementary medical treatments, and visits to faith healers and energy workers – along with the best modern medicine has to offer in treatment and palliation.

Along the way, I have benefited from a variety of healing companions, from whom I've learned much about healing in shared healing ministry and creative dialogue, whether in person or print: Morton Kelsey, Susan Trout, John Harvey Gray, Mary Jane Pagan, Larry Dossey, and Dale Matthews. I am grateful for their insights and guidance in the areas of healing and wholeness.

I am grateful to my publisher Henry Neufeld and editor Jody Neufeld for their support and editorial assistance, respectively. I am thankful to Bob Cornwall, a faithful and insightful pastor, for introducing me to Energion Publications. I am thankful beyond words to two friends, both of whom have faced health challenges, Anna Rollins and Patricia Adams Farmer, whose reading of the text reminded me that the pathway to healing goes through the valley of the shadow and not around it!

My life has been enriched by two faith communities, concerned with healing and wholeness, Georgetown University Protestant Ministry and Disciples United Community Church (Lancaster, Pennsylvania), as well as several congregations and denominational groups with whom I have led retreats and taught classes. I am grateful for their generosity along with the insights of my students at Lancaster Theological Seminary and Wesley Theological Seminary.

My faith has been challenged and strengthened by loving relationships with friends and family facing serious and life-threatening illnesses with whom I've practiced healing prayer, reiki healing touch, and personal and communal laying on of hands. From them, I've learned that love is at the heart of healing. Through it all, I have grown in spirit, love, and insight with my partner in life, ministry, and parenting for over thirty years, Katherine Gould Epperly.

May everyone who reads this text be blessed with God's healing touch in body, mind, spirit, and relationships. May we all discover God's abundant life in every moment of living and dying, and experience God's healing touch that transforms cells and souls, and enables us to experience healing even when a cure is no longer possible. As scripture proclaims, "nothing can separate us from the love of God in Christ Jesus our Lord."

Epiphany 2012

CHAPTER ONE

An Invitation To Healing

My Journey to Healing. The healings of Jesus have always been a part of my life. As a young child growing up in the Salinas Valley of California, I often sat with my mother on Sunday afternoons, watching television and enthralled by the sensual voice and diaphanous gowns of Kathryn Kuhlman as she purred, "I believe in miracles." I was often startled by Oral Roberts as he slapped people on the forehead and shouted "Be healed." From these early television healers, I heard testimonies of bodies healed and lives transformed. I learned that God was concerned with healing, and that God was most powerful when we were most vulnerable.

In an era before HIPAA regulations regarding patient privacy, I often accompanied my father, the local Baptist minister in our small town, on his pastoral calls and hospital visits. I was my "father's boy" and in the course of our pastoral visits or in sitting in hospital waiting rooms, I overheard stories of pain and anguish and listened to my father praying for God's healing presence to be made manifest in the lives of vulnerable people. Sometimes those prayers were answered and his congregants returned to their previous lives with vigor and purpose; but other times it appeared that God had turned a deaf ear to our pleas or, as we often rationalized, had better things in mind for us. After all, we believed that this life was the front porch to eternity and death was the doorway to everlasting life. But, such explanations didn't make sense, even to a child, when people survived serious illness and the "better things" involved paralysis, pain, senility, and death. Even as a young child, I wondered how God could be so powerful, and let bad things happen to people I loved.

As a preacher's kid, I lived in world of celebration and desolation. Looking back at over thirty years of ministry, I now realize how much death and illness defined my father's pastoral work and how often as a pastor and friend I have sat at the bedside with people facing surgeries and incurable illnesses. In my childhood church and home, we rejoiced in the birth of children and mourned at the sudden death of a young parent, a fatality from an automobile accident on Highway 101, or a cancer diagnosis that meant only one thing in those days – a slow and painful death.

When I was eight years old, my mother began to suffer from depression and what later would be called obsessive compulsive behavior and obsessional ideation. She sought medical treatment, received electro-shock treatments, was hospitalized on two occasions, and struggled bravely, personally and professionally, for the next three decades. Although mental health issues were in the closet in those days, I heard my mother cry out to God in her emotional pain and vulnerability. I still hear echoes of her plaintive cries for a miracle that others – at least on television – seemed to regularly receive with very little effort on their part. I suspect that as the years went by, my mother saw her delicate mental health as being similar to the apostle Paul's "thorn in the flesh" and like Paul, she soldiered on, returning to college to update her degree and then elementary school teaching for twenty years before retirement. I believe that my mother received a healing – the ability to go on despite her fears and anxiety – although she never experienced a cure or respite from the inner conflicts and phobias that shaped her – and my – day-to-day life. Maybe with Paul, she came to realize that in our weakness we can experience God's sustaining companionship and strength (2 Corinthians 12:7-10). I know now that only by prayer and trust in God did my mother get up each morning to face the voices of unruly children and her own inner chaos. Though I didn't realize it at the time – and few children do – my mother was a hero of faithful persistence, fighting her "demons" by the grace of God with all the courage she could muster one moment at a time.

I heard of miraculous cures – described as dramatic and supernatural – from the testimonies televised on Sunday afternoon religious programs. My father even claimed to have taken the diagnosis of a second hernia to God's "mercy seat," prayerfully asking God to deliver him from pain and hospitalization. Although he didn't publicly claim a cure, my dad revealed to me that the pain ceased and the hernia was healed. He gave thanks to God when his physician pronounced that there was no longer any need for the surgery that would devastate our family's finances and, in those days, debilitate him for several weeks.

As I said earlier, the life of a pastor's family and pastoral ministry in general is punctuated by occurrences of illness, debilitation, and death. As a young boy, already inclined toward theological reflection and mystical experiences, I pondered in my own naïve way the perennial questions of faith: "What did it mean to say that Mr. Clemons was living on 'borrowed time?' Why did the rifle go off just as my classmate Billy Thompson was pulling it out of his father's car after a day of hunting? Why did the school custodian recover from surgery while a neighbor lady died 'under the knife?' Why were our prayers answered in one case, but apparently rejected in another?" I was not content with the typical answers I heard from adults – "it was God's will" or "God answers our prayers with 'yes', 'no', or 'maybe'." They seemed either evasive or insensitive to my young theologian's mind. Still, I prayed and continued to be intrigued by the antics and miraculous claims of the Sunday afternoon healers.

In the wonderfully direct way of children, I prayed about everything and often my prayers led to tests of faith, especially as I prayed for concrete events such as retrieving lost baseballs in my backyard, my team's victory in the World Series, a Sunday school teacher's recovery from surgery, and for my Mom to feel better. My prayers in those days were simple and without guile, "God help the Pittsburgh Pirates win" or "God help Arnold Palmer make the winning putt," "Let Mom be happy," or "Make Mrs. Beebe get well."

While I never tabulated the results of my prayers, I remember that I was disappointed on a regular basis when my prayers weren't immediately answered. I hadn't yet learned to be patient with prayer and to recognize that our prayers are seldom answered in a linear cause and effect manner, but fit into a larger context of what scientists call "quantum entanglement" and ecologists call the "interdependence of life." Nevertheless, I kept on praying. I couldn't avoid thinking about prayer, because prominently affixed to our refrigerator door was the motto, "Prayer changes things." Every time I searched for a snack, I was encouraged to consider the power of prayer! Even to a young child, the kitchen motto begged the question: does prayer have any power at all to transform human life in its painful complexity?

I suspect my experiences mirror those of many other Baby Boomers raised in evangelical and Pentecostal environments. Our lives were saturated with prayer and images of Jesus' healings. We sang songs like "Pass Me Not, O Gentle Savior," "Sweet Hour of Prayer," "Amazing Grace," "Just as I Am," and later "He Touched Me." Even when we rebelled and left the faith of our childhoods, as many of us did to follow the pathways of Asian religions, countercultural lifestyles, and political protest, we still had a fascination with mysticism, prayer, and paranormal experiences. You might say that my interest in healing was bred to the bone in that Baptist parsonage, and that regardless of how far I wondered from my childhood faith, I was still a God-believing Baptist child at heart. Although my personal and professional desire to understand Jesus' healings would evolve in the context of learning spiritual practices related to traditional Chinese medicine, yoga, Transcendental Meditation, alternative and complementary medicine, and reiki healing touch, every step in my global healing adventure led me closer to claiming as an adult the importance of Jesus' healing ministry and the power of the New Testament healing stories to transform peoples' lives.

As I entered graduate school and prepared for the ministerial and teaching professions, I no longer viewed the healings of Jesus from the perspective of televangelists like Oral Roberts and Kathryn Kuhlman or their successors Benny Hinn and Richard Roberts. While I began to doubt the integrity and veracity of many of the televangelists and their accounts of miraculous cures, I knew that some of the vulnerable and simple people in their healing lines experienced temporary, if not long term changes, in their overall well-being. In contrast to the spectacular claims and gaudy sets of the televangelists, I rediscovered the importance of Jesus' healing ministry in simple acts of compassion, prayer, and healing touch. The healing stories of Jesus' ministry came alive to me not as supernatural violations of the cause and effect processes of nature or as magical changes we could instantly call upon by our prayers or force of will, but as images of hope that inspired me day after day to seek wholeness and healing for myself, those whom I loved, strangers, and world events. I saw – and still see – most healing as gradual and subtle in nature. I discovered that love was the key to healing, even when a physical cure is unlikely.

The point of this preamble is both confessional and affirmative. As an adult I reclaimed the healing stories of the Bible. Like the words of the Corn Flakes commercial, I wrestled with these stories "again – for the first time." This time, however, my perspective was far more global than my Baptist upbringing. Although that evangelical child still lives within me, shaping my relationship with Jesus as companion and friend, I reclaimed the healings of Jesus through my encounters with Christian mysticism, complementary and technological medicine, process theology, quantum physics, Biblical scholarship, and reiki healing touch, a form of hands on healing that promotes well-being by balancing and intensifying the healing energy of the universe.[1] I found that Jesus' healings are part of much larger movement toward healing, reflecting God's quest for abundant life for people of every continent, faith, and ethnicity. My experiences have shaped my vision of first and twenty-first century

1 For more on reiki healing touch, see Bruce and Katherine Epperly, *Reiki Healing Touch and the Way of Jesus* (Kelowna, British Columbia: Northstone Press, 2005).

healing. I also rediscovered Jesus the healer – and still am jour-
neying on this healing frontier – in the midst of my own need for
healing and transformation, chronic and life-threatening illnesses
of friends and family, my son's diagnosis and recovery from cancer,
and my responsibilities as a pastor and spiritual leader, called to
pray with people in crisis, vulnerability, infirmity, grief, and despair.

I've experienced Jesus' healing touch in hospital rooms, healing
services, energy work, spiritual conversations, and simple heart-felt
prayer. Healing will always remain essential to my faith, but the
quest for healing will always be challenging to me, personally, theologically, and spiritually. I suspect that healing is mysterious and
challenging to you as well even if you consider yourself a person of
faith who believes in the power of prayer to change bodies, minds,
spirits, and relationships.

**Rediscovering Jesus the Healer in the Modern and Post-
modern Worlds.** Interest in healing has peaked in recent years.
Until the last few decades of the nineteenth century, Jesus' healing
ministry was consigned to fringes of Christianity. As Morton Kelsey
insightfully recounts in *Healing and Christianity*, the healings of
Jesus were marginalized within a few centuries after Jesus' ministry as the church, facing the realities of persecution and plague,
focused peoples' attention on the afterlife.[1] This world was viewed
as the testing ground in the grand conflict between God and Satan
for eternal possession of the souls of humankind. What did a few
healthy years matter when your life is suspended by a thread above
the flames of hell? Further, the unambiguous message of God's love
proclaimed by Jesus was eclipsed by church teachings that identified
sickness with divine punishment, correction, and decision-making.
The great Christian teachers – Augustine, Aquinas, Luther, Calvin,
and Zwingli– saw Jesus' healings as peripheral to the message of
God's graceful forgiveness of sinners that opened the floodgates of
salvation to undeserving humanity. Radically different in tone and
overall message from the Reformation gospel, the proponents of

---

1 Morton Kelsey, *Healing and Christianity* (Minneapolis: Fortress Press,
1995).

philosophical deism, the belief that the divine clockmaker created the world and then let it move forward on its own accord without intervening, continued the marginalization of Jesus' healing ministry and the healing ministry of the church. Deism attracted many intellectuals and influenced how orthodox Christians viewed God's relationship to the world. Deism consigned divine activity to the margins of human life, leaving the important temporal decisions to us. Any intervention by God would have to be from the outside rather than from within the predictable world of cause and effect. Among believers of all theological persuasions, the image of a deistic God encouraged the belief that God acted supernaturally from the outside, answering prayers or intervening to prevent tragedies or harm our enemies without consideration to the regular patterns of cause and effect that govern our lives. Despite the contrast between the Living God of scripture and the Spectator God of deism, popular Christianity began to see God as a "personal being," or "individual" standing beyond the world of change who could only come into our lives from the outside supernaturally in law-defying ways. This led to a further separation of mind and body and faith and medicine in responding to issues of health and well-being.

It is just a small step from deism to the belief, widely held among more liberal theologians and clergy for last two centuries, that the healings of Jesus were entirely metaphorical or moral in nature. The healing stories were intended to be invitations to spiritual transformation and acts of hospitality, changing people's status from unclean and unwanted to clean and accepted in the social order. In either case, God's business was primarily with spiritual lives and ethical conduct of persons and not the physical world of sickness and health. Whereas liberals exorcised the healings of Jesus from their understandings of faith, believing that issues of health and illness should be left to medicine and not the church, many fundamentalist Christians saw healing as essential to the spread of the first century gospel but no longer relevant to the church's mission of saving souls. They believed that God's focus in this historical dispensation, or period of history, is soul winning, not physical or political transformation.

Still, Christ can never be pinned down by our worldviews or theologies. People in need seek wholeness and in the process discover surprising healing energies that can't be explained by theologies that restrict God's actions solely to bygone eras, spiritual well-being, and occasional supernatural events. Interest in Christian healing reemerged in the late nineteenth century, first, among followers of Mary Baker Eddy's Christian Science movement and the "mind cure" philosophies that influenced her understanding that health and illness are direct reflections of our spiritual condition without any relationship to our illusory bodies.[1] Eddy believed that God has given us a "science" to promote healing. Correct thinking and optimism lead to good health; negative thinking is manifest in illness. Cures can only occur at the spiritual level, since ultimately our perception and affirmation of the reality of the physical world is the result of turning from divine perfection. If you focus on the eternal truths of Divine Mind, immersing yourself in the propositions of Eddy's *Science and Health* and the guidance of a Christian Science practitioner, the illusory ills of embodiment will fade away. Today, many contemporary new age approaches to healing, such as those found in the writings of Louise Hay, *A Course in Miracles,* and the best-selling *Secret,* reflect Eddy's belief that health and prosperity are entirely a matter of our mental and spiritual state.[2] Spiritual truth alone is necessary for well-being: change your thoughts and your body and financial situation immediately will change for the better. Conversely, all illness is self-caused, a result of fear, alienation, and negativity.

Shorty after Eddy's discovery of Christian Science, revival fires broke out on Azuza Street in Los Angeles, California, and then

---

1 Mary Baker Eddy, *Science and Health with Key to the Scriptures* (Boston: The Christian Science Board of Directors, 1994).

2 See Louise Hay, *You Can Heal Your Life (Los Angeles: Jay House, 1999); Rhonda Byrne, The Secret* (New York: Atria Books, 2006); *A Course in Miracles* (Mill Valley, CA: Foundation for Inner Peace, 1975).

across the North America and the world as groups of Christians affirmed that the church was on the verge of a second Pentecost, characterized by the Holy Spirit's movements through speaking in tongues, healing, paranormal experiences, and miraculous acts of power and prophesy. Rather than focusing on the mind as the source of healing and spiritual transformation, Pentecostals affirmed the lively presence of God's miracle-working Spirit coursing through all things, and providing spiritual, financial, and physical deliverance for people in need. Faith no larger than a mustard seed could open the pathways of divine healing that Jesus' first followers experienced. Experiential in nature, the Pentecostal movement justified its affirmation of Jesus' healing ministry by pointing to peoples' life-changing encounters with the Holy Spirit. The healing ministries of Oral Roberts, Kathryn Kuhlman, and later Benny Hinn as well as the prosperity gospel and "name and claim it" movements carried the Pentecostal message of miracle and healing to the wider world of television, radio, and "big tent" and auditorium ministries.[1] While different in philosophy from Christian Science, the new age movement, and Science of Mind, many Pentecostal healers also connected spiritual states, often in a direct and unilateral way, with issues of health and sickness, and prosperity and poverty. In extreme forms, "faith healing" placed the burden of health entirely on vulnerable people many of whom could not, even by force of will, conjure up the mustard seed faith prerequisite to God's supernatural interventions.

Healing ministry reached mainstream Christianity through the ministries of Agnes Sanford, Olga Worrall, and Morton Kelsey. These mainstream pioneers recognized God's presence in the Pentecostal experience, first described in Acts of the Apostles, and located that experience in the context of the rational, theologically-reflective, and organized worship styles of moderate Christians. Today, virtually every denomination has, at least, some marginal interest in

---

1 Harvey Cox, *Fire from Heaven: The Rise of Pentecostal Spirituality and the Reshaping of American Religion in the Twenty-first Century* (Cambridge, MA: Da Capo Press, 2001).

healing ministry, mostly in the context of spiritual formation and medical ministries. Almost every denominational worship book or supplementary resource contains healing liturgies for individual and communal worship. While avoiding supernatural explanations for healing, many mainstream and evangelical Christians see God as the source of healing who desires our well-being, and invites us to be part of a healing process that includes prayer, medicine, and community support.

Healing Movements in the Twenty-first Century. Interest in the healings of Jesus gained momentum as a result of the rise of complementary and alternative medicine, the transformation of Western medicine to embrace the role of spirituality in health and illness, growing scientific evidence of the role of religious practices in promoting overall well-being, and the changing face of Christianity and the growth of Pentecostal spiritualities in the Southern hemisphere. In the next few paragraphs, I will briefly describe the current spiritual context that shapes our understanding of Christian healing and invites us to explore and embody the healings of Jesus with renewed vigor.

First, complementary and alternative medicine has become mainstream in many North American hospital settings. As a result of the impact of global medical and spiritual practices, many major hospitals have courses and practitioners in Tai Chi and Qigong, Reiki healing touch, massage and still touch, mindfulness meditation, visualization, stress reduction, and yoga. In my own work as a medical school professor, the growing interest in complementary medicine has amazed me: in the 1980's when I showed videos on Chinese medicine, my first year medical students were skeptical; a decade later, they wanted referrals to acupuncturists and energy workers. I was even given the opportunity to teach courses on spirituality and religious pluralism to medical residents in psychiatry, typically the most agnostic of the medical specialties. I found that these young psychiatrists recognized the role of faith in psychological health and pathology, regardless of their own personal beliefs.

What is unique about complementary medicine is that, in contrast to much Western medicine, which until recently separated issues of mind and body and spirituality and health, complementary medicine affirms the importance of spiritual practices, mental attitude, and relationships to our well-being and the ultimate energetic realities of the universe. For many people, their first encounter with spiritual practices occurs in the hospital or at medical appointment and not at church. The rise of complementary medicine and its emphasis on the role of spirituality in health and illness creates a bridge between twenty-first century medical treatment and Jesus' healing ministry. Jesus is no longer viewed as an ancient magician, employing folk remedies and drawing upon peoples' superstitions. In fact, Jesus' approach to healing is seen by many complementary health practitioners as employing some of the same practices that are emphasized in complementary medicine and the growing integration of East and West in medical treatment: prayer and meditation, healing touch, faith, positive psychology, acceptance, hospitality, psychological techniques, and the transfer of healing energy from healer to patient. In recent years, when I've advised a stressed out congregant to begin a spiritual practice, such as centering prayer or quiet contemplation, he or she often responds with the comment, "I recently received the same advice from my doctor."

Second, medicine is embracing the spiritual as well as physical in diagnosis and treatment. Once characterized by mind-body dualism and its focus solely on the body, Western medicine has come to accept the importance of spirituality in health and illness. Physicians have always recognized the mysterious "will to live" as a significant factor in recovery from illness. Today, many doctors also recognize the importance of responding to the whole person, not merely in terms of her or his body, but also in prevention, treatment, and ongoing care. For example, stress has been found to be an important factor in a variety of diseases from hypertension and heart disease to acne and cancer. Personal experience and medical research suggests that the stresses of life are as much a reflection of our attitude, perspective, and faith as the impact of work, family life, and economics. Scientists have discovered the wisdom of Jesus, who invited his followers to "consider the lilies" and trust that God would care for their deepest needs. Spiritual practices such as meditation, mindfulness training, and transformed attitudes toward time, work, and success have been integrated into medical treatment plans.

This creative synthesis of high tech and high touch opens the door to recognizing the importance of spirituality in promoting well-being, whether at home or in the hospital setting. The gospels depict Jesus taking time for prayer and retreat (Mark 1:35-39; 6:30-46). Paul reminds his congregations to seek spiritual and mental transformation and focus on virtues rather vices, in other words, affirmative faith or positive thinking (Romans 12:2; Philippians 4:8-9). The emergence of the "faith factor" in health and illness testifies that the wisdom and power revealed in Jesus' ministry can transform the spiritual, emotional, and physical lives of twenty-first century persons. Indeed, many physicians make it a practice to ask their patients if they would like a prayer prior to surgery or during an office visit.

Third, science is studying the sacred and has discovered God in our cells as well as our souls! While once objective medicine focused on the body alone and discouraged religious practices in the hospital setting, except in terms of pastoral care of patients' nebulous "spiritual needs," today scientific studies indicate that practices such as prayer and meditation promote physical as well as spiritual well-being. Moreover, religious commitment, measured in terms of church involvement and personal values, has been identified with a variety of positive health outcomes ranging from reduced hypertension, lower rates of substance abuse, greater longevity and quality of life, and more rapid recovery from surgery.[1] Virtually no one contests that value of the relaxation response, most often

---

1 Harold Koenig, *The Healing Power of Faith* (New York: Simon and Schuster, 2001); Dale Matthews, *The Faith Factor: The Proof of the Healing Power of Prayer* (New York: Penguin, 1999).

elicited by forms of prayer and meditation, in reducing stress and anxiety and their impact on physical and emotional well-being.[1]

While more controversial, a variety of medical studies have identified intercessory prayer, that is, praying for others, as promoting better recoveries and a reduced need for medication following heart surgery. The impact of prayer on plants, grasses, and other non-human organisms has been studied to eliminate the impact of the placebo effect – the influence of faith and expectation – associated with human subjects. Presumably, plants, grasses, and mice don't have the faith that can interfere with more linear medical research! In the majority of these cases, prayer has been identified as a factor in the healing of wounds in mice and the growth of grasses. These ground-breaking studies have led to the emergence of a new medical mottos to go along with the new medical models, emphasizing the interconnectedness of mind, body, spirit, and relationships: the faith factor (Dale Matthews), prayer is good medicine (Larry Dossey), religion is good for your health (Harold Koenig), and the molecules of emotion (Candace Pert).[2] The growing evidence and practice of whole person, or holistic, mind, body, spirit, medicine creates a bridge between the first and twenty-first centuries. The One who proclaimed "your faith has made you well" may well have been referring to physiology as well as spirituality!

Fourth, the changing face of Christianity in the twenty-first century opens the door to recognizing that faith involves mysticism and Pentecostal experience as well as rationalism.[3] European and North American Christianity – and in this geographical category I also include Australia and New Zealand – has lived with the ambiguous influence of the modern world view and its skepticism

1 Herbert Benson, *The Relaxation Response* (New York: Mass Market Paperbacks, 1976) and *Beyond the Relaxation Response* (New York: Mass Market Paperbacks, 1985).
2 Larry Dossey, *Healing Words: The Power of Prayer and the Practice of Medicine* (San Francisco: Harper One, 1995).
3 Philip Jenkins, *The New Christendom: The Coming of Global Christianity* (Oxford: Oxford University Press, 2011).

about anything remotely mystical, non-rational, or supernatural. Influenced by Enlightenment rationalism and the scientific method and their emphasis on naturalistic, observable, and this-worldly causes, mainstream biblical scholars and seminary-trained ministers have often sought solely naturalistic and scientific explanations for the healing stories of the New Testament. From this perspective, Jesus' healings were described as the products of superstition or myths with no bearing in reality as we understand it, products of the placebo effect, or made up stories to give credence to Jesus' unique relationship to God, which itself was questionable in a one-dimensional, tightly deterministic cause and effect world in which miracle and magic alike are incomprehensible. Courses on healing and spirituality were seldom found in mainstream seminary curricula, despite the anecdotal evidence of congregants, pastors, and seminary students who experienced answers to prayer and surprising health improvements as a result of prayer or laying on of hands. Among many mainstream pastors in the last half of the twentieth century, it was assumed prayer might reduce tension or provide spiritual comfort, but it surely had no impact on our physical conditions. Many of these pastors implicitly lived by renowned biblical scholar Rudolf Bultmann's critique of the healing stories of the gospels: anyone who turns on an electric light must see the miracles of Jesus as superstitious vestiges of a bygone era.

Narrow understandings of the relationship between prayer, health, and divine power are being questioned, in part due to the growing theological and spiritual liberation of Southern hemisphere Christianity from the rationalistic bias of the Northern hemisphere. While healthy faith involves both rationalism and mysticism, what the great theologians of the church described as "faith seeking understanding," a truly holistic and life-transforming faith embraces the growing Pentecostalism of the Southern hemisphere and the mysticism of Quaker and Celtic spiritualities along with the creative agnosticism and rationalism of Northern hemisphere religion and the scientific method. The fastest growing Christian communities are below the equator, and these communities take healing, spiritual gifts, answers to prayer, and mysticism seriously. As more and more people move from south to north, along with the growing Latino/a population in the United States, the face of European and North American Christianity is changing not only in complexion, ethnicity, and language but also in worship style, spiritual practices, and openness to miraculous events. This growing shift in Christianity is an invitation to a creative synthesis involving theological reflection, spiritual practices, and Pentecostal and mystical experiences in our emerging understanding of Jesus' healing ministry. This synthesis joins the insights and practices of Pentecostal Christians, Western-trained physicians, complementary health care givers, scientists and researchers, and mystically-oriented mainline, emerging, and progressive Christians. Today, we can affirm in light of science and medicine that the dynamic healing powers described in the Gospel of Mark and the New Testament witness can be factors in bringing wholeness to vulnerable humankind.

Mark's Healing Gospel. Written sometime between 65-75 C.E., Mark is the earliest of the written gospels. In many ways, Mark's simplicity and directness define what a gospel should be; not an exact chronological account, complete description, or objective report of clearly datable events, but a theological document, similar to a sermon, whose purpose enables people to understand, experience, and be transformed by encountering the good news of Jesus Christ and God's reign of Shalom or wholeness. The Gospel of Mark and its successors (Matthew, Luke, and John along with the non-canonical gospels) are intended to create and sustain faith in Jesus and enable readers to experience the power and grace which comes from a relationship with God's beloved child. This is truly good news – to encounter the living Christ, still healing through his liberating word, welcoming actions, and healing touch.

Although we don't know the identity of the author of Mark's Gospel, many scholars suspect that it was a younger companion of either Peter or Paul. Mark drew his narrative of Jesus' life from oral and written materials circulated among the first Christians.[1] No doubt, like the other three biblical gospels and the many extra-canonical accounts of Jesus' life,[2] the author whom we call "Mark" emphasized certain aspects of Jesus' ministry and placed others in the background, as a result of his theological perspective, understanding of Jesus' identity and mission, and awareness of the needs of the communities he was addressing. Some scholars believe that Mark's emphasis on the interplay of healing and suffering in the life and ministry of Jesus are intended to encourage and empower Christian communities undergoing persecution, primarily at the hands of violent Roman oppressors.

Mark, like the other gospels, gives us a glimpse of Jesus' life and ministry, and not the whole story. Indeed, if we look specifically at the healing stories, none of them can be encompassed by the written word. How can we describe what happened to the woman with the flow of blood in the short paragraph included in the gospel? Her experience – or that of Jairus and his family – leap from the page into our hearts, hands, and imaginations, inspiring us to be God's healing partners and good news bearers in our time. As John's Gospel proclaims, "There are also many other things that Jesus did; if every one of them were written down, I suppose that the world itself could not contain the books that would be written" (John 21:24). God's wisdom, embodied in the healer from Nazareth, is always more than we can imagine or fathom. No paragraph-long story can encompass the intricate tapestry of fear, hope, and amazement that characterize every gospel healing narrative or our own quests for healing and wholeness.

Mark's intent is to invite us to experience the good news of Jesus by giving us a portrait of his acts and teaching. The heart of

---

1 See the bibliography for texts on Mark's Gospel.

2 Some of the non-canonical gospels include the Gospel of Thomas, Gospel of Mary, Gospel of Judas, Pistis Sophia, and the Gospel of Philip. For more on these gospels, see Elaine Pagels, *The Gnostic Gospels* (New York: Viking Press, 1989).

Mark's gospel can be found in his description of the first days of Jesus' ministry:

> *Now after John was arrested, Jesus came to Galilee, proclaiming the good news of God, and saying, "The time is fulfilled, and the kingdom of God has come near; repent, and believe in the good news" – Mark 1:14-15*

For Mark, the good news involves Jesus' healing of mind, body, spirit, and relationships and our openness to being transformed by God's coming reign. It inspires turning from the ways of death to the path of life. Mark's Jesus is truly a holistic healer whose teaching and touching changes physiology, social standing, and spiritual values. When Jesus cures someone, everything changes in her or his life – he or she moves from outcast to beloved friend; guilt is released and physical ailments spontaneously disappear; touch awakens life-transforming energies. Every cure points beyond itself to Shalom or wholeness, the primary characteristic of God's realm and vision for our world, then and now.

Mark is a healing gospel, not just because it contains at least seventeen miracle and healing stories or because nearly half of the first eight chapters pertain to healing and illness, but because Mark intended his first listeners and their communities as well as readers like ourselves to experience healing in the act of reading and contemplating the stories themselves. Mark intended the gospel to be read imaginatively and with a sense of wonder. Every story in its brevity leaves out important details, not only by Mark's intention, but to enable us to use our imaginations to see ourselves as characters in the story. Like every inspired author, Mark gives us space to shape the story itself for our needs and the challenges of our time. Every reader of Mark's Gospel, without exception, and this includes Mark himself as he reflected on the oral traditions he received, needs healing in some aspect of her or his life and virtually every spiritual, physical, and emotional condition finds voice in Mark's simple narrative. The Gospel of Mark is intended to reach out to every person and every spiritual, physical, emotional, or relational condition with the promise of God's healing love.

Like the rest of the New Testament, Mark's Gospel was meant to be read by communities and not just solitary individuals. Mark is clear that the realm of God, the embodiment of God's values in everyday life, requires communities devoted to healing and wholeness; it also calls forth healing communities dedicated to transformed relationships at every level of life – individual, marital, familial, relational, congregational, communal, and planetary. We are to replicate in our congregations and relationships the healing circle that Jesus created to bring healing to Jairus' daughter or the courageous faith of four friends who tore open a roof to seek healing for their friend. Communities need to hear and believe that they can experience good news, be transformed, and then transform the world. We need to hear Jesus' loving words to Bartimaeus, "What do you want me to do for you?" as an inspiration to reflection, confession, and bold petition for the healing of ourselves and our loved ones.

Although my focus is primarily the meaning of Mark's healing gospel for people today, I also call upon the wisdom of John's Gospel. The last of the four gospels to be written, probably near 100 C.E., John's Gospel complements the starkness and straightforwardness of Mark: John is philosophical, Mark is concrete; John is global, Mark is local; John's Jesus is a philosophical teacher, Mark's Jesus is a hands-on practitioner. John describes the heavens and the resurrected life, while Mark points to resurrection emerging in our daily lives, as we are astounded by wonder of personal transformation and overwhelmed by an empty tomb and an absent body. In that spirit, I will focus on John 5 and John 9, the healings of the man at the pool and a sight-impaired man, to address the profoundly personal as well as theological issues of sickness and suffering. Amid their apparent contrasts in approach, method, and attitude toward healing (John has the fewest healing stories), both Gospels share the belief that those who truly encounter Jesus Christ are radically changed and renewed: energized by God's healing presence, they shall mount up with wings of eagles, running without weariness, and walking with strength (Isaiah 40:31).

Theology and Healing. The healings of Jesus challenge us to join faith and knowledge in order to be responsible interpreters of the texts. As a theologian, who reflects on questions of God, suffering, meaning, prayer, revelation, and virtually everything human, one of my tasks is to explore what healing and wholeness mean in the twenty-first century.

We live in a very different world than the first Christians: our names for diseases differ as do our diagnostic and treatment protocols. Maladies attributed in the first century to demon possession, while not ruled out by modern theology or science, are now primarily understood in terms of physiological or psychological causes, and treated with medication, counseling, and psychotherapy. Modern understandings do not necessarily challenge the gospel healing stories but frame them in light of our time, place, and technology. The healing stories don't stand still, but come alive in new and creative ways from generation to generation.

Theologians ask hard questions of scripture, spiritual healers, and scientists to fathom the complexities and impact of personal and intercessory prayer, positive thinking, community support, personal choices, and God's presence in health and illness. I regularly challenge liberals, evangelicals, new agers, and Pentecostals alike in my explorations of faith, healing touch, prayer, and spiritual energy. I believe that peoples' lives are transformed by the interplay of call and response, reflected in the dynamic interplay of God's presence and our own religious practices. I still must ask the same hard questions that surfaced in my own childhood, though with the recognition that theologians, like physicians, must follow the principle, "first do no harm."

As a believer in God's healing presence in our lives, who regularly participates in liturgical healing services, reiki healing touch sessions, and prayers of intercession and petition, I am compelled to ask questions such as: Where is God in this situation? Why did God cure one person but not the other? Is God responsible for the pain and grief we experience? How do we judge some of the dramatic healing claims – restoration of the dead and growing of new limbs - made by both Pentecostals and new agers? How do we explain failure in ways that do not blame the victim or her or his family? How shall we understand these healing events in light of our contemporary understandings of medicine and medical treatment?

A theologian must ask challenging questions to insure that our religious explanations heal rather than harm. In many healing contexts, persons with illness and their parents are still blamed for their illness or their failure to improve. In other cases, people are told that God gave them unendurable pain or debilitation to strengthen their character, test their faith, teach them a lesson, or punish them for sins. Along with everyday believers, theologians challenge explanations that lack adequate moral, spiritual, scientific, or intellectual stature and gravitas.

Theology begins with the question of suffering and the profound distance between our hopes and dreams and the stark realities of moral imperfection, sickness, oppression, injustice, and death. Theology can add to the suffering of the world through superficial or harmful explanations of peoples' conditions. But, it can also be a healing force, enabling people to open to powers within and beyond themselves and to balance the realism of their current prognosis with the deeper realism of God's loving presence coursing through our cells as well as our souls. My questions – and yours as well – are not the result of faithlessness but a testimony to our desire to be faithful to God's wisdom and spiritually sensitive to vulnerable and suffering people. As you reflect on Mark's healing gospel, bring your whole self to the text, in the spirit of a loving father who confessed, "I believe; help my unbelief."[1]

My Approach to Mark's Healing Gospel. Good theological reflection involves the interplay of vision, promise, and practice. It

---

1 For more on the theology of healing, see Bruce Epperly, *God's Touch: Faith, Wholeness, and the Healing Miracles of Jesus* (Louisville: Westminster/John Knox, 2001) and *Healing Worship: Purpose and Practice* (Cleveland: Pilgrim Press, 2006).

also involves embodiment and emotion. Our words must take flesh in acts of justice, love, and healing. Accordingly, my approach to Jesus' healings involves heart, mind, and hands. I see the healing stories as an invitation to our own personal healing and wholeness. I don't assume that we should take these stories literally without questions, doubts, and second thoughts, nor should we assume that we can replicate them exactly in our time. We live in what singer-songwriter Paul Simon describes as an age of miracle and wonder technologically in which we join prayer and Prozac, contemplation and chemotherapy, and intercession and intravenous drips. We have tools for treatment and palliation that no one in Jesus' time could imagine.

Still, we deal with the realities of sickness and mortality. These realities shape our quest for healing and our hopes for divine assistance when our own efforts no longer avail. I believe that God is at work in the world in the cells of our bodies and in our spiritual adventures. I write as a believing scholar, who seeks to practice what I preach and experience the words I write in the dramatic and undramatic moments of everyday life. Like my father and mother before me, I have a prayer list of persons in crisis for which I intercede every day. I daily visualize people surrounded by God's healing light and transmit healing energy through reiki healing touch. I regularly lead and participate in healing worship services. Still, I struggle to understand the meaning of healing and God's role in healing and illness. I take time to pray throughout the day, yet I live with unanswered prayers on a daily basis. I will share my experiences with healing and illness in the course of this book and invite you to reflect on your own encounters with God during life's most vulnerable moments.

In the course of conceiving, researching, and writing this text, two of my closest friends have died of cancer, one whose life was interwoven with mine for over forty years, the other a fellow parent and next door neighbor whose son was one of my son's best friends. I prayed whole-heartedly for them, bringing my intercessions to what my Baptist parents called "the throne of God" in quest of a cure. Right now, three other close friends are facing diagnoses of incurable cancer. One has just refused further medical interventions beyond palliation, entered hospice care, and prayerfully waits for her death, trusting in God's promises. The other, my dearest friend and spiritual companion is facing a new cycle of chemotherapy and radiation treatment. Just this morning, I received word that one of my wife's oldest friend's wife recently died after a ten year battle with breast cancer. Her pastor-husband is dealing the pain of bereavement like the women who came to Jesus' tomb that first Easter morning.

As you read this text, I invite you to bring your whole self to Jesus' healing stories. Place yourself in the text as you seek to fathom its intellectual, spiritual, emotional, and vocational meaning for yourself, your loved ones, and your community. Each chapter weaves together scriptural study, theological reflection, spiritual practices, personal narratives, and practical application.

Each chapter will conclude with a spiritual practice related to the healing story being considered. Feel free to shape these practices according to your personal and spiritual needs. I also include questions and spiritual practices for group study and spiritual formation at the end of the book.

In conclusion, let me once again state that this book is a labor of love and a testimony to prayer, building on nearly thirty years of living with the healings of Jesus as a pastor, theologian, spiritual guide, and person seeking my own healing. May you experience God's healing touch and transforming love and seek to embody God's healing marks in your own life.

CHAPTER TWO

TRANSFORMING FAITH

When Jesus had crossed again in the boat to the other side, a great crowd gathered round him; and he was by the lake. [22]*Then one of the leaders of the synagogue named Jairus came and, when he saw him, fell at his feet* [23]*and begged him repeatedly, 'My little daughter is at the point of death. Come and lay your hands on her, so that she may be made well, and live.'* [24]*So he went with him. And a large crowd followed him and pressed in on him.* [25]*Now there was a woman who had been suffering from haemorrhages for twelve years.* [26]*She had endured much under many physicians, and had spent all that she had; and she was no better, but rather grew worse.* [27]*She had heard about Jesus, and came up behind him in the crowd and touched his cloak,* [28]*for she said, 'If I but touch his clothes, I will be made well.'* [29]*Immediately her hemorrhage stopped; and she felt in her body that she was healed of her disease.* [30]*Immediately aware that power had gone forth from him, Jesus turned about in the crowd and said, 'Who touched my clothes?'* [31]*And his disciples said to him, 'You see the crowd pressing in on you; how can you say, "Who touched me?"'* [32]*He looked all round to see who had done it.* [33]*But the woman, knowing what had happened to her, came in fear and trembling, fell down before him, and told him the whole truth.* [34]*He said to her, 'Daughter, your faith has made you well; go in peace, and be healed of your disease.'*

While he was still speaking, some people came from the leader's house to say, 'Your daughter is dead. Why trouble the teacher any further?' [36]*But overhearing what they said, Jesus said to the leader of the synagogue, 'Do not fear, only believe.'* [37]*He allowed no one to follow him except Peter, James, and John, the brother of James.* [38]*When they came to the house of the leader of the synagogue, he saw a commotion, people weeping and wailing loudly.* [39]*When he had entered, he said to them, 'Why do you make a*

commotion and weep? The child is not dead but sleeping.' [40]*And
they laughed at him. Then he put them all outside, and took the
child's father and mother and those who were with him, and went
in where the child was.* [41]*He took her by the hand and said to her,
'Talitha cum', which means, 'Little girl, get up!'* [42]*And immediately the girl got up and began to walk about (she was twelve years
of age). At this they were overcome with amazement.* [43]*He strictly
ordered them that no one should know this, and told them to give
her something to eat. – Mark 5:21-43*

A Helpless Parent. I know how Jairus felt when he sought out
Jesus to heal his daughter. One Saturday evening in October 2007,
I received an unexpected call from my daughter-in-law. My recently
married son had been experiencing respiratory discomfort for a
few weeks. He had seen the college physician, who believed it was
bronchitis, but despite medication, he continued to have symptoms
of lung congestion and discomfort. Not satisfied with the diagnosis
and experiencing no improvement despite medications, he decided
to go into the emergency room to have it checked out. The X-rays
revealed a large mass in his chest. When I received the word, I was
shocked and devastated. My unspoken response was "he's going to
die." My next response was "how will I tell my wife Kate?" who was
at the time on a spiritual pilgrimage in Iona, Scotland.

That was one of the longest twenty four hours in my life as I
tried to contact Kate, pack my things, and drive from Lancaster,
Pennsylvania to Washington D.C. As I drove to the hospital, all I
could stammer was a silent prayer of desperation, the traditional
Kyrie Eleison, "Lord, have mercy. Christ, have mercy. Lord, have
mercy." A saga began that week that would include MRI's, CT
scans, blood tests, physician visits, and chemotherapy. While the
treatment was successful and my son is now the parent of a healthy
toddler, the apple of his grandpa's eye, with another on the way, I
will always bear the marks of facing his life-threatening illness. Like
Jairus, I believed that our children are supposed to outlive us. When
they are sick, our instinct is to protect them and trade our lives for
theirs. I'm sure that's how Jairus felt as he bowed down before the

healer Jesus, desperately begging for a cure. While he was used to sending emissaries to do his bidding, the severity of his daughter's condition compelled Jairus to forget his pride and social standing, and bow down before the miracle worker.

In a blink of an eye, everything can change. As Susan Sontag says, each of us has two passports, one for the land of the healthy and the other for the land of sick. I am sure that Jairus and his wife had dreams for their twelve year old daughter. I am sure that, as upper class Jews of the first century, they anticipated a good marriage and children and a rich and full life of Sabbath dinners and playing with the grandchildren. Now, everything they had hoped for was on the verge of slipping away.

The Life-changing Reality of Chronic Illness. Illness can come upon us suddenly, but it can also be chronic, plaguing us day after day with pain and inconvenience, always lurking in the background and shaping our every move. Even on good days, when we almost forget our health condition, there is a nagging whisper, "when will the shoe drop again, when will the pain return, when will I be embarrassed or debilitated by my condition?" Many of us live with chronic conditions, ranging from well-controlled hypertension (my own chronic ailment) to Crohn's disease, HIV/AIDS, arthritis, and even cancer. We may not die from them but we will die with them as our companions. We are never quite well, even on good days. There is, as one elder noted, the reality of "not so good days and bad days."

Chronic illness can constrict our reality and limit our activities. We live in the "meantime," hoping for a few moments of respite and longing for a cure to what we must endure or fear will eventually kill us without advances in medicine. Our schedule is punctuated by visits to our physicians, daily medications, and medical tests. What was once unusual has become the new normal. Even if we have good health care insurance, our out of pocket expenses may deplete our savings and leave us living from month to month. The dream of a happy retirement, spending time with our grandchildren, and traveling across the world is swallowed up by the daily nightmare of pain, infirmity, and limitation. Simple tasks like gardening, wrapping Christmas presents, walking down the street, or controlling our bowels become monumental, devastating, and often embarrassing.

Our loved ones are also forever changed by our health conditions. They must adapt, alter their expectations, and become caregivers and protectors as much as companions. As Simone de Beauvoir confessed as she witnessed her mother's debilitation and dying process, the whole world shrunk to the size of her hospital room. Surely that was how the woman with the flow of blood felt as day after day, in fact, over 4,300 days, twelve years, she endured the discomfort, isolation, and hopelessness of chronic illness.

Yearning for Healing. Healing can occur at any place and time. Even when we're not expecting it, we can become channels of God's healing touch. As Jesus rushes off to respond to Jairus' plea, a woman also hurries to see the healer. Her illness was more than inconvenient; in her culture, it had rendered her a social outcast. Her pain was not just physical, but emotional, relational, and spiritual. A woman with a chronic flow of blood, likely gynecological in nature, was condemned for a lifetime of loneliness in the "red tent." According to the holy books and religious laws, she was considered unclean not just in her menstrual cycle but every day of her life. Everything she touched was contaminated, and that included her husband and random passersby. Just listen to these words from Hebraic law:

> *If a woman has a discharge of blood for many days, not at the time of her impurity (menstrual cycle), or if she has a discharge beyond the time of her impurity, for all the days of the discharge she shall continue in uncleanness; as in the days of her impurity, she shall be unclean. [26]Every bed on which she lies during all the days of her discharge shall be treated as the bed of her impurity; and everything on which she sits shall be unclean, as in the uncleanness of her impurity. [27]Whoever touches these things shall be unclean, and shall wash his clothes, and bathe in water, and be unclean until the evening. [28,31]Thus you shall keep the people of*

Israel separate from their uncleanness, so that they do not die in
their uncleanness by defiling my tabernacle that is in their midst.
– Leviticus 15: 25-28, 31

Even God found her reprehensible and threatening, according
to her religious tradition. She could not engage in sexual intercourse
nor could she go to religious services. If she and other unclean people marred the purity of synagogue precincts, God might withhold
God's presence from worship and turn away from the community's
prayers.

According to many religious observers, and perhaps even Jairus, the leader of the local synagogue, she was sick for a reason: she
had done something wrong and was now receiving divine punishment for her misdeeds. After all, many people, including people of
faith, look for explanations for life's tragedies. Einstein once noted
that "God doesn't play dice." The issue of suffering is as old as Job
and, though we will address the problem of pain and illness later
in this text, no doubt this woman felt the judgment of her peers.
She may even have internalized the moral judgments of others,
retreating into guilt and shame for an illness she had not caused.
Deep down, she may have come to believe that she was solely responsible for her illness, and deserved the pain and ostracism that
was her daily reality.

Many readers assume that this woman was in midlife or beyond in terms of our modern life expectancies, but the text gives no
clear information about her age. Perhaps, she was only twenty four
or twenty five. When she was Jairus' daughter's age, just beginning
puberty, she may have experienced a life-changing gynecological
ailment. With her whole life ahead of her, she found herself condemned to isolation, loneliness, and contempt. I believe that the
fact that Mark does not mention her name points to his recognition that in contrast to Jairus, she had no social standing or honor
within the community.

As she rushed from her home in search of the healer, she may
have wondered, "Would he reject her, too? Would he recoil at her

uncleanliness, fearing that she might contaminate him? Would he judge and rebuke her?" But, something keeps her from giving up. Something propels her forward despite the dirty looks from by-standers and possibility of rejection by the healer. Deep within, in that place of "sighs too deep for words," a divine possibility urged her onward and, despite years of despair and hopelessness, gave her courage and hope for a cure.

The limitations we face can be the womb from which possi-bilities are born. That day, one thought emerged and pushed to the forefront of her mind that enabled her to risk everything in the quest of healing. "If I but touch his clothes, I will be made well." You can imagine her repeating this over and over as a mantra or an affirmation to give her hope and courage. She may have considered turning back when she saw the crowd gathering around the path the healer would be taking. But, these words, "if I but touch his clothes, I will be made well," guided and strengthened her resolve as they lured her forward toward the realization of the hopes and prayers of twelve years.

The Energy of Love. When she touches Jesus, a power goes forth. We can't describe what happened. It goes beyond the exper-tise of physicians, theologians, and Bible scholars. But, I believe that the energy of the universe, the power that gave birth to the big bang fourteen billion years ago, flowed from Jesus to her. The scriptures call this lively inner energy, *dunamis*. Other religious traditions describe it as *ki, chi*, or *prana*. By whatever name, it is the energy that gives life, birth, and blessing. This energy flows through us every moment of our lives, refreshing our souls and our cells. It is the energy of growth, imagination, immunity, and healing, described in John's Gospel as the lively sap that flows from vine to branches (John 15:4-7). In that moment, there was a quantum leap of this universal energy flowing from Jesus to her and her whole being, body, mind, and spirit was transformed.

Agnes Sanford, a pioneer in healing ministries within the Epis-copalian tradition and mainstream Christianity, speaks of God's healing light being similar to the flow of electricity through our homes. It is always present, but we need to plug into it to benefit from its power to heat and illuminate. This unnamed woman connected to God's healing energy through her faith. By her faithful affirmation, she opened to new dimensions of reality which enabled God's power to flow more dynamically, healing her body, mind, spirit, emotions, and relationships. In her case, her faith called forth God's healing touch, creating a field of force that enabled God to be present in a dramatic and life-changing way. Later Mark describes the faith of other sufferers whose friends placed them along Jesus path:

> *And wherever he went, into villages or cities or farms, they laid the sick in the marketplaces, and begged him that they might even touch the fringe of his cloak, and all who touched it were healed. – Mark 6:56*

This woman's faith was essential to the cure she experienced. But nothing would have happened apart from the energy of love in which we live and move and have our being (Acts 17:28). Mark affirms that Jesus is the focal point of God's energy of love. In reaching out to him, even without his conscious awareness, a power was released to restore her to personal, social, and religious well-being. No doubt, the woman is amazed by the unexpected power she is feeling. She is overwhelmed by a dramatic change in her cells as well as her spirit. She may even have wanted to run away to let the experience sink in. But, when Jesus calls her forth, she courageously steps forward one more time, in fear and trembling, but also gratitude and praise.

Who knows what she tells Jesus? But his response captures the intimacy of God's love for this ostracized woman and for each of us: "Daughter, your faith has made you well; go in peace, and be healed of your disease." You are clean now, not just physically healed, but spiritually and socially restored. You will never be an outsider again. You never were to begin with, for God has always loved you. Hold your head up high, walk forward courageously,

and have a great life in the years to come. In calling her "daughter," Jesus is welcoming her into God's realm, the family of God in
which we are all clean and worthy regardless of our health condition
or previous social standing.

She heard his words, "daughter." Though she was no theologian, she experienced the meaning of God's graceful omnipresence.
The God of the universe is also the Companion of Every Soul. As
Augustine noted, "God loves each one of us as if there is only one
of us." How long had it been since someone called her name with
such intimacy and care? For years, she had been addressed in pity
and derision, but now she hears words of love. She was no longer
a social outcast, but a member of God's realm, healed and whole.
Former Speaker of the House Tip O'Neill once stated that "all
politics is local." The same is true for theology and doctrine. Our
theological beliefs about God, human life, sin, grace, and the world
have little value unless our words become flesh in life-transforming
ways. This ostracized woman felt firsthand the divine compassion
of which the scriptures spoke. She experienced God's incarnation in
the world – the embodiment of divine wisdom and creativity - in
a loving voice and surprising energy.

A World of Contrasts and Similarities. The gulf between
Jairus and this unnamed woman was almost unbridgeable. He
was an insider, she was an outsider. He was righteous, she was
considered a sinner as a result of her sickness.[1] He was clean, she
was unclean. He was wealthy, she was on the verge of destitution.
He could go anywhere, she was restricted in her movements. Yet,
sickness is the great leveler. When we find ourselves in the land of
sick, we may receive different treatment, according to the quality
of our health insurance and disposable income, but we are all alike

---

1 In the biblical tradition, the word "sin" is more than a moral judgment,
it refers to anyone who falls outside the categories of social approval and
inclusion whether based on health condition, behavior, occupation, or
ethnicity. For more on first century Jewish images of "sin" and "sinners,"
see Greg Carey's *Sinners: Jesus and His Earliest Followers* (Waco: Baylor
University Press, 2009).

in our fear, uncertainty, and vulnerability. The mortality rate has always been 100% whether you wealthy or impoverished, notable or overlooked. Eventually all of us will face the realities of death and diminishment over which we have little or no control.

As he witnessed the encounter between Jesus and the woman, Jairus may have experienced a conversion of heart. Previously, he may have looked down upon this woman as a threat to the purity of the community. He may even have warned his daughter about people like her. He might have judged her as unclean, sinful, and deserving of her precarious health and economic condition. He may have uncritically echoed the religious mores that assumed that she had brought her condition upon herself as a result of undisclosed ethical misconduct. But, now he and his little daughter were in the same boat. Perhaps, some of his colleagues may have suggested that some misdeed on his part led to his daughter's illness. His desire to protect his daughter and to insure her survival and flourishing, trumped any judgments he might have had. As the African-American spiritual proclaims, he knew that both he and this now-transformed woman were "standing in the need of prayer," living in hope for transformation that transcends human effort, and can only be experienced through the synergetic power of God's call and our response.

Healing Circles. How many of us have heard a handful of words that change everything in our lives? Earlier this year, I received an email reporting that one of my dearest friends, Wendy, had just died of a brain tumor. We had known each other since high school. She was my erstwhile girlfriend in the early 1970's and one of the few people in my life who "knew me when." We had communicated regularly after her diagnosis until she was beyond any communication except prayer. In the months prior to her diagnosis, we had two lovely dinners and enjoyed the sights and sounds of the Pacific Ocean near her home. I couldn't imagine that this vibrant spirit would be taken from my life and the world.

Only a few months later, I discovered my older brother lying dead in his mobile home a few miles from where I live in Lancaster,

Pennsylvania. Prior to that moment, I had never experienced a day without my brother in my life, and now as the holidays come and go, his absence is overwhelming at our holiday table. I had just talked to him twenty minutes before and rushed to his house to respond to what he described as a panic attack, and now he was gone. He will never sit with us at Thanksgiving dinner or eat plates of nachos and chili on Super Bowl Sunday.

I know how Jairus felt when he heard the words, "Your daughter is dead. Why trouble the teacher any further?" Death shatters our dreams for the future. It rends the fabric of relationships and places our beloved beyond our care and intimacy. But Jesus is an all-season healer. He never abandoned anyone in need, and he would not abandon Jairus and his family despite the crowd's consensus that she was beyond his power. At that moment, Jesus, like many pastors, knew he was needed more than ever, either to console grieving parents or to rouse by his prayers and divine power this child from a coma the neighbors confused with death. You may notice that I believe that Jesus' recognition that she was sleeping, not dead, makes the story all the more powerful. The word "sleep" can be a euphemism for death, but it may also point to a comatose condition. Regardless of her state, Jesus is confronted with a moment of decision: Will Jesus trust the crowd's diagnosis that she is dead and beyond our care? Or, will he look deeper, open to the possibility that she may be comatose or that he might be able to provide the spiritual CPR that will bring her back to life? In either case, if Jesus had abandoned her even for a short time and trusted the crowd's negative judgment, she would have surely died.

Jesus does something radical, similar in spirit to his cleansing of the Jerusalem Temple. He bars the door to everyone who assumes the situation is hopeless. More accurately, he tosses the naysayers out. He creates a healing circle, comprised only of the parents and three of his disciples. These become his team of healing companions, strengthening his power and ability to access God's healing energy by their faith and love. While I do not believe that our prayers can be quantified, such that finding two hundred intercessors will be more effective than twenty in curing an illness, I trust the scriptural affirmation that when two or three persons are gathered in faithful openness, marvelous things can happen. The heavens can open up, and the powers resident in our cells and souls can burst forth. This is not a violation of the causal relationships of nature, but a reflection of the dynamic synergy of God and the world. God is present in every cell, and certain moments may activate God's healing energy in life-changing and dramatic ways.

A Many-faceted View of Sickness, Health, and Healing. In the spirit of systems thinking, holistic health, and process theology, I believe that health and illness are the result of many causes – ranging from lifestyle, diet, economics, attitude, to our spiritual life. They are also influenced by our prayers, faith, and the faithfulness of others as well as God's personal call to wholeness and abundant life. Physicians have called this "the faith factor," revealed in the impact of our faith and religious commitments on our well-being and recovery from illness.[1] Most of the time, recovery emerges from the interplay of faith, medicine, and our body's immunological resources. But, in rare moments, the confluence of God's presence and our faith enables greater healing energies to emerge that can change bodies and spirits. We can't control such moments, nor are they arbitrary actions of a God who chooses some rather than others for physical cures. Jesus' mission statement proclaims God's care for each of us: "I have come that they might have life, and have it abundantly" (John 10:10). But, the nature of abundant life is contextual and intimate, and shaped by a variety of factors, including our environment, social situation, beliefs, the prayers of others, and our overall health condition.

Faith matters! God calls us toward abundant life, health and well-being, every nanosecond. As Revelation 3:20 proclaims, "Listen! I am standing at the door knocking; if you hear my voice and open the door, I will come in to you, and eat with you, and you with me." When we open to God's moment by moment vision of possibilities, new energies and inspirations burst forth to heal mind,

---

1 Dale Matthews, *The Faith Factor* (New York: Penguin, 1999).

body, and spirit. The energy of God's vine, described in John 15, flows through us making us "fruitful" in energy, hope, and wholeness. Even if we do not experience a physical healing, and we can never guarantee a cure despite our faithfulness and spiritual stature, we may discover the courage to face what cannot be changed. We may experience an emotional and spiritual healing that enables us to face death and disability knowing that God is with us and is moving in our lives, enabling us to be strong in our weakness and faithful in our vulnerability.

More than once in my career as a pastor, I have encountered people who have been healed, despite the fact they were never cured. They ministered to me, deepening my faith and restoring my soul, in their pain and weakness. I recall my pastor-father, now confined to wheelchair and living in a nursing home, looking up at me and saying in a barely audible voice, "I'm stuck. But it's ok." He was vulnerable and isolated, but his faith in God helped him endure each day with a smile and a word of kindness to his caregivers. He was never cured, but he felt the peace that passes understanding. His witness inspires me to believe that I can face life's most challenging situations with the awareness of God's loving presence. You can be healed without being cured and, sadly, cured without a healing if you remain imprisoned by fear, addiction, and alienation despite being in great physical shape.

Faith Matters! Our faith matters not only to our loved ones and those for whom we pray, it matters to God. Our openness to God shapes the nature and intensity of God's presence in our lives and the world. How else can we understand, the surprising words of Mark 6:1-6:

> He left that place and came to his home town, and his dis-
> ciples followed him. ²On the Sabbath he began to teach in the
> synagogue, and many who heard him were astounded. They said,
> "Where did this man get all this? What is this wisdom that has
> been given to him? What deeds of power are being done by his
> hands! ³Is not this the carpenter, the son of Mary and brother of

James and Joses and Judas and Simon, and are not his sisters here
with us?" And they took offence at him. ⁴Then Jesus said to them,
"Prophets are not without honor, except in their home town, and
*among their own kin, and in their own house." ⁵**And he could***
do no deed of power there, except that he laid his hands on
a few sick people and cured them. ⁶And he was amazed at
their unbelief. *(my emphasis)*

While we cannot defeat God's ever-present aim at healing,
wholeness, and shalom, we can stand in its way, diluting its impact
on our lives. God always acts concretely and intimately, addressing
our needs and attitudes in this and not another world. God never
addresses humans in the abstract, but human beings right where
they are in all their complexity of belief and unbelief. Mark's Gospel
clearly asserts that we are active agents, possessing a degree of power
and responsibility in relationship to God and in our health condition. Mark recognized that we are not passive victims or clay to
be manipulated without our consent. God cherishes and supports
our agency. The potter respects the properties of the clay even when
he or she is forming a vessel. Our life situation, like the properties
of the clay, shapes how the Divine Artist works in our lives. God
wants us to stand up and walk, and not sit on the sidelines in terms
of our health condition or future prospects.

We have a role in our healing process. We are neither impo-
tent nor omnipotent. Our faith can make us well, but prior to any
faith on our part, God is already at work in our lives, inspiring us
to seek wholeness amid the limitations of life. In Nazareth, the
faithlessness of the town folk limits what Jesus can do, but it does
not fully nullify his power. As Mark notes somewhat wistfully, "he
could do no deed of power there, except that he laid his hands on
a few sick people and cured them. ⁶And he was amazed at their unbelief." These are not words of threat, just a statement of fact; they
are also an invitation to an adventure in healing and wholeness.
If faithlessness can impede God's activity in our lives, faithfulness
can open new pathways for divine energy and inspiration to flow
into our lives. Within the concrete limitations of life – and this is

what incarnation is all about – God presents us with possibilities and the energy and inspiration to achieve them. When we open the door through personal and community prayer, meditation, faithfulness, and action, miracles – acts of power, transforming persons and communities – happen. Our faith activates in a healing way what scientist Candace Pert describes as the "molecules of emotion," which are not restricted to our brain but are found in our stomach, intestines, and throughout our body. Our faith can be embodied in the transformation of cells in such a way that it can lead to unexpected cures, relief from pain, greater energy, or greater longevity and quality of life for persons with incurable diseases.

Who Belongs in Your Healing Circle? When he arrived at Jairus' home, Jesus did not work alone, nor should we. Healing is seldom linear or unilateral. God acts through the world of relationships, tenuous as they may be at times. God works through you and me to bless those around us. Jesus assembles a team of five, inspired by faith and love.

When our son was hospitalized, we sent out notes to our healing partners – colleagues, congregants, friends, and relatives – and they passed the word on to others. People we never met - and probably never will meet - took time each day for prayers that our son would respond to the chemotherapy. I believe that these prayers along with our faith and hope created a field of force that enhanced my son's immune system and the impact of the chemotherapy. This was not magic, or contrary to the way the universe works, but reflected our faith in a God whose love gives birth to galaxies and whose care embraces cancer cells and chemical agents. We believe that God was present in the commitment of nurses, technicians, chemists, and physicians such as Nancy Dawson, Larry Einhorn, Ed Tsou, Jim Gordon, and Robin Gross who treated our son. As physician Dale Matthews asserts, God heals through prayer and Prozac or, in our case, contemplation and chemotherapy, supplication and cisplatin.[1]

---

1 Cisplatin is a platinum-based chemotherapy treatment, in my son's case, part of the BEP protocol for mediastinal testicular cancer, bleomycin, etopiside, and cisplatin.

The story of Jairus' daughter begs the question: Who is your healing team? Who would you take in the hospital room with you if your situation was desperate? Whose faith inspires you to have greater faith? Whose hope inspires you to be hopeful? Whose initiative challenges you to become an actor, when you are tempted to passivity and victimization? In other words, who is your personal church, your two or three companions gathered in the healing God's name?

Conversely, who are you called to support in times of challenge? Who needs your healing touch and word of affirmation? Are there persons who look to you as their beacon in the darkness and anchor in the storm?

It's All About a Meal. Healing is always intimate and personal. Jesus once again speaks words of intimacy and care, "*Talitha cum*, little girl get up." In a world in which children were often expendable, Jesus had a special concern for children and although this girl was twelve years old and almost on the verge of adulthood, she was still in his eyes an innocent, vulnerable child. Then and now, Jesus blesses the children that governments, congregations, and businesses neglect. As I write these words, two miles from our home in Lancaster, Pennsylvania, my wife Kate is sitting with our friend Kharga as his wife Bhagi gives birth to their first child. Kharga became a family member when our church sponsored him and his Bhutanese family through Church World Service.[1] I am certain that God is blessing this little Hindu child. As a child I remember singing, "Jesus loves the little children, all the children of the world, red and yellow, black and white, they are precious in his sight." In five days it will be Christmas and as I think of this newborn child and my (then) sixteen month old grandson, I am synchronously listening to the hymn "Once in Royal David's City":

For he is our childhood's pattern,
    day by day like us he grew;
he was little, weak and helpless,

---

1 For more on Church World Service, see www.churchworldservice.org

tears and smiles like us he knew.
And he feeleth for our sadness,
    and he shareth in our gladness.

In this Christmas hymn and in Jesus' intimacy with an unnamed woman and girl, and all the vulnerable, neglected, and
ostracized people of the world, we experience the lived meaning of
what otherwise are irrelevant theological abstractions: God's omnipresence and omniscience. God is right where we are, whether
in good health or at the descending edges of life. God's presence
is in the hospital room, at the graveside, and in chemotherapy
treatments. That's what omnipresence means! God knows us fully,
seeing us through the eyes of love. Dietrich Bonhoeffer asserted
that "only a suffering God can save." I am certain that the healer
Jesus was touched by the anxiety in Jairus' voice and the tears in
his wife's eyes. I believe that Jesus felt the relief and joy that the
recently-healed woman experienced. Healing comes from God who
is touched by our longings, prayers, and pain. God is not, as the
philosopher Aristotle proclaimed, "the unmoved mover," whose
perfection is found in his distance from the world's pain. No, God
feels our pain and joy. Jesus shows us God as "the most moved
mover," whose openness to receive all of our feelings shapes God's
activity in the world. That's what omniscience means!

When Jairus' daughter awakens, she begins to walk around,
perhaps, amazed at her recovery and delighted in simple pleasures
of movement, sight, and sound. But, the healing is not complete.
Jesus tells them to "give her something to eat." These are odd words.
At first glance, I wonder why Mark includes them in his account
of this healing. But, then, I realize that healing is all about a meal,
a celebration of life. On that day, it wasn't just any meal. It was
the meal of new life and resurrection for this girl and her family. I
suspect Jairus and wife immediately thought of her favorite foods
and set to work on preparing them for her. Celebrate, my daughter
is alive, let's have a party!

Do you remember how good a meal tasted after you recovered from the flu, surgery, or completed chemotherapy treatments? Do you remember how refreshing water or ginger ale can be when you're sick? Do you recall gathering with friends and family for special events? As I review this text on a cold wintry morning, I am recovering from a stomach virus, and am looking forward, like that young girl, to a healthy and delicious meal, once I recover! Take a moment right now or later today to imagine the following: *You have just awakened after facing a difficult illness. You are feeling renewed and refreshed, and then happy to discover that Jesus is your companion. Jesus looks lovingly at you and asks, "What would you like me to cook for you?" How would you respond? What foods would satisfy your soul as well as your body, freshly made in the kitchen of the Chef Jesus?*

Healing is Eucharistic. It inspires a meal in which God is our guest and our companions are honored. It inspires the raised glass, the joyful toast, the alleluia, and hymn. Hosanna! Praise God for a young girl's life and a woman's restoration.

HEALING MARKS

Good theology involves vision, promise, and practice. It portrays a world in which God is alive and moving through the cells of our bodies, our relationships, and the commitments of health care givers, first responders, and all who stand on the side of health and justice. The theology of Mark's Gospel portrays God as the source of health and wholeness. But, it also asserts that we are actors in the healing process. What we do makes a difference to God and our neighbors. In the spirit of Jewish mysticism, we are called to God's partners in *tikkun 'olam*, healing the world.

This and every chapter ends with a practice to enable us to become actors who embody what we've just read. You may personalize them in any way that is helpful to you, but take them seriously as ways of opening the door to Christ's presence in your life.

The scriptures are filled with short affirmative statements that have the power to widen our horizons, transform our lives, and open us to greater manifestations of God's healing energy in our lives. The woman with the flow of blood found the courage to reach out to Jesus by focusing her attention on the words, "If I but touch his clothes, I will be made well." They became a mantra that she repeated over and over again as she pushed her way through the crowd. Jesus created a healing circle for a young girl by inviting only those who had hope in her recovery to stand by her bedside.

Do you recall the story of Peter walking on the water? As long as he focused on Jesus, he could do what he previously assumed to be impossible. But, the moment he wavered in his vision, letting his attention be dominated by the storm rather than Jesus' steadfast love, he sunk like a stone. Affirmations are not a denial of reality, whether our financial, relational, or physical condition, rather they are positive statements that place illness and pain, and anxiety and social stigma, and other life conditions, within the context of the larger reality of God's presence and power in our lives. The waves may splash over us as they did Peter, but Jesus is our companion, and we will be safe. There is danger, but there is also support and protection.

The use of affirmations has the power to change our minds, first, consciously, and then, in the depths of the unconscious, where many of our fears and self-imposed limitations lurk. In healing both the conscious and unconscious, we awaken to a world of wonders, possibilities, and healing energies. Surely this is what the apostle Paul means when he counsels the Philippians to "think about these things" – justice, honor, purity – and then makes two affirmations about how the perception of the world changes when we see our lives from God's standpoint:

> *I can do all things through God who strengthens me.*
> *– Philippians 4:13*
> *My God will fully satisfy every need of yours according to his riches in glory in Christ Jesus. – Philippians 4:18*

Paul recognized that we can change our lives by transforming our attitudes toward the events we experience.

Be not conformed to this world, but be transformed by the renewing of your mind. – Romans 12:2

Affirmations heal our minds, push the boundaries of the possible, and open us to God's healing energies. We still have challenges but we face them with God as our companion, guide, and protector. As you look at your quest for healing and wholeness, consider what affirmations you need to live by these days.

One way to discover these affirmations is to enter a time of prayer and meditation. First, pause for a few minutes, gently observing your breath as you center yourself in God's presence. Prayerfully ask the following questions: What is my greatest personal need today? Where do I need healing in my life? What words of wisdom will awaken me more fully to God's healing presence in my life? Take several minutes to listen deeply to the inspirations of the Spirit. As words or images emerge, frame them in short positive statements.

For example, you may discover a need for greater patience, courage, or physical well-being. You may need to move from passivity to action. These affirmations might emerge from your life situation:

> I have all the time, energy, and money I need
>   to flourish and serve God.
> In Christ, I am brave and strong.
> God's healing touch rests upon me.
> I can do all things through Christ who strengthens me.

In the course of the day, regularly repeat your affirmations, especially when you are succumbing to negative feelings. A friend of mine was terrified of an upcoming surgery. While it was not life-threatening, the idea of going under anesthesia was overwhelming to her. In the week before her surgery and, later, as she was wheeled into the operating room, she felt a peace that amazed her. She was experiencing the meaning of the affirmation she had lived with for the past few weeks: Nothing can separate me from the love of God.

I have an early morning coffee affirmation. A dear friend of mine gave me one of a pair of handmade coffee cups, knowing that the first thing I do each morning, after my morning prayers, is make a cup of coffee. As I take the first few sips I say a prayer for her and my family. Although she wakes up later than I do, she practices the same affirmative routine that joins us spiritually. This is especially powerful these days as my friend is being treated for cancer.

Each morning as I go out for my three mile walk, I begin my journey reciting the words of the Psalmist, "This is the day that God has made and I will rejoice and be glad in it." Regardless, of what I am facing, this biblical affirmation frames my day and shapes my perception of the world. This is God's world, God is working in my life and in the lives of those I meet, and I will encounter the world with joy.

CHAPTER THREE

God, Why Am I Sick?

As he walked along, he saw a man blind from birth. ²His disciples asked him, "Rabbi, who sinned, this man or his parents, that he was born blind?" ³Jesus answered, "Neither this man nor his parents sinned; he was born blind so that God's works might be revealed in him. ⁴We must work the works of him who sent me while it is day; night is coming when no one can work. ⁵As long as I am in the world, I am the light of the world." ⁶When he had said this, he spat on the ground and made mud with the saliva and spread the mud on the man's eyes, ⁷saying to him, "Go, wash in the pool of Siloam" (which means Sent). Then he went and washed and came back able to see. – John 9:1-7

Later Jesus found him [the man who had been ill for 38 years] and said to him, "See, you have been made well! Do not sin anymore, so that nothing worse happens to you." – John 5:14, excerpt from John 5:1-18

Steve came into my study with a troubled look on his face. He slumped in one of the wing chairs and began to pour out his heart to me. "I've just gotten the news. I've been diagnosed with testicular cancer. I'm afraid, embarrassed, and angry. This is the second cancer I've had in the last ten years. What have I done wrong? Why is God punishing me? I feel like Job right now. God has forsaken me, or maybe it's all a sham – my faith, my attempts to be a good person, my hard work haven't gotten me anywhere. I cry out to God but no one's answering." Carrie and Tom felt the same divine absence and arbitrariness when their first baby miscarried. They had just started going to church and had made a commitment to living a Christian life. They were good people before joining the church, but during the first several years of their marriage God was irrelevant to them. They focused on getting ahead, buying a nice home, and having all the toys that are treasured by young professionals – a luxury automobile, Kindle and iPad, iPhone, entertainment center, and home in the right neighborhood. They came to me devastated both emotionally and theologically. They wondered if God was punishing them for their consumerism and for living together before they were married. Tom articulated what they both were thinking, "Are we being punished for living together before we got married? We didn't hurt anyone. In fact, we were doing what everyone else did. Why us? Is God somehow out to get us for a few sins we committed? Surely God wouldn't kill our baby just because we lived together before getting married."

More often than I'd like to admit, I have received papers from undergraduate students or heard explanations in the media that state that "there's a reason for everything that happens." When we or someone else experiences a tragedy, many of us want to know why. We don't like to live in a world where God plays dice or events happen randomly and for no apparent reason. We want clarity and predictability. We want to be able to chart a clear cause and effect relationship between what's happened today and our previous actions, whether this involves a terrorist act, the diagnosis of a life-threatening illness, an auto accident, or a job loss. Life is messy and complicated. But, when evil befalls us, many of us can't imagine a world of sheer randomness and chance. We want our suffering to mean something or fit into the wide scheme of things – whether in protecting our country, helping our family, promoting the evolution of the species, or divine decision-making. The quest for a reason for the suffering we have experienced has led to the most inspirational and insightful as well as the most superficial and harmful theological reflection.

Two healing stories from John's Gospel – the man who had been born blind and the man who had sat 38 years waiting for a miracle – provide a window into Jesus' understanding of the why we get sick and how we can become well again. Jesus did not attempt to provide a systematic theology of healing in these passages or elsewhere. In fact, Jesus' theology emerged in the messiness of human relationships and not the solitary equanimity of an ivory tower. But, Jesus' words and actions help us eliminate some of the most personally and theologically harmful explanations for the suffering we experience and provide a pathway toward the healings we so desperately need.

Explaining Evil. It has been said that theology begins where the pain is, and both of these stories emerge out of lifelong experiences of pain, judgment, and exclusion. Guilt is written all over the story of the man who was born blind. From the safe perspective of personal well-being, the disciples ask, "Who sinned, this man or his parents that he was born blind?" No doubt the disciples held some version of the acts-consequences or rewards-punishments understanding of health and illness, found in Leviticus 26. Put simply, those who follow God's rules are blessed, while those who deviate from God's commandments are cursed. Consider how the man born blind and his parents must have felt as they heard these words read in the synagogue, if the man and his parents were even allowed to attend:

> But if you will not obey me, and do not observe all these commandments...I in turn will do this to you: I will bring terror on you, consumption and fever that wastes the eyes and cause life to pine away. – Leviticus 26:14-16
>
> If you do not diligently observe all the words of this law that are written in this book, fearing this glorious and awesome name, the Lord your God, then the Lord will overwhelm both you and your offspring with severe and lasting afflictions and grievous and lasting maladies. – Deuteronomy 28:58-59

"Where did we go wrong that our boy can't see?" they may have asked themselves.

Others might have assumed that they were suffering the consequences of some sin, hidden from the public eye. Some might even have thought the man himself must have committed a sin prior to his birth that led to a lifetime of blindness. They might have justified his suffering with the words of Psalm 51:5: "Indeed I was born guilty, a sinner when my mother conceived me." As they encountered this family, passersby, especially those who were enjoying the fruits of their labors and good health, might have complacently justified their well-being with the words of Deuteronomy:

> *If you only obey the Lord your God by diligently observing all his commandments.... Blessed shall you be in the city, and blessed shall you be in the field. Blessed shall be the fruit of your womb, the fruit of your ground, and the fruit of your livestock, both the increase of your cattle and the issue of your flock. Blessed shall be your basket and your kneading bowl. – Deuteronomy 28:1, 3-5*

Put starkly, the healthy and wealthy deserve their prosperity and well-being, while the sick and impoverished are responsible for their pain and destitution. Sadly, even today, this form of acts-consequences thinking shapes political and economic rhetoric. The wealthy, even those who inherited their wealth, are entitled to their largesse and to low tax rates. On the other hand, the poor must justify any social or educational consideration. How often have political leaders implied that the poor are lazy and exaggerated the impact of welfare fraud while neglecting the impact of the more socially-destructive white collar crime on social and economic well-being!

Who sinned? Why am I suffering, God? Throughout the centuries, philosophers and theologians have sought to explain both good and bad fortune. While we often take for granted our good fortune, sickness, job loss, and personal reversals demand an explanation. For those who believe that the universe and personal life is guided by an intelligent, powerful, and loving being, explaining our suffering becomes acute – a matter of faith and doubt, and belief and unbelief.

The most obvious explanation for the suffering we and others experience is that we deserve it. We are simply reaping what we've sown whether in this or a previous lifetime. With the growing impact of Asian religions and new age philosophies, the concept of karma, cause and effect in the course of many lifetimes, is often invoked to explain inequalities in birth and talent. Good and bad fortune in terms of our births, physical condition, and talents are the result of the positive or negative impact of actions from a previous lifetime on our current life. From this perspective, this man is blind because of some misdeed in a previous lifetime or a lesson that he needs to learn in this lifetime. Perhaps, some new age spiritual leaders suggest, he failed to "see" the pain of others in a previous lifetime and must, in this lifetime, experience what it's like to be blind and the subject of other's pity and neglect.

While few Christians believe in reincarnation, many implicitly follow a linear version of the acts-consequences approach to health and illness, success and prosperity. Following the terrorist attacks on 9/11, many preachers suggested that God had withdrawn God's shield over the United States as a result of its moral relativism. Others asserted that Hurricane Katrina hit New Orleans because of its toleration of homosexuality, despite the fact that the lively and welcoming French Quarter suffered virtually no significant damage. On a personal level, some baby boomers believe that today's illnesses reflect God's just punishment for their sexually promiscuous and ill-spent youth of drugs, sex, and rock and roll.

The notion of linear cause and effect in health and illness has become a landmark of new age as well as "name it and claim it" theologies. In both cases, the quality of our faith or spiritual life directly determines our overall well-being. More than once, I have counseled Christians whose pastors have told them that "if you have more faith your daughter will get well. Your daughter is ill because of your faithlessness and immorality." Similarly speaking, the popular new age text, *The Secret,* claims that there is an exact one-to-one correspondence between the quality of thoughts and the events of our lives. We create our own realities by our positive or negative thinking. Along with wealth, healthy relationships, and physical well-being, rape, cancer, heart disease, and poverty reflect our spiritual state.

Now, we can't discount the impact of lifestyle, thought patterns, faith, and morality on the health of persons and nations even over the course of generations. Our current economic crisis is not accidental, but the result of greed, financial misconduct, and ineffective regulatory systems. A lifetime of smoking may lead to emphysema and lung cancer, not to mention the impact of second hand smoke on children's health. Parents' level of education is a significant factor in their children's health. Unemployment is related to increase incidents of substance abuse and domestic violence, all of which shape the health and well-being of spouses and children. Yet, some have prospered, including dishonest business people, during the recent recession, while faithful Christians have lost their jobs and faced foreclosure. Negative thinking and anxiety can depress our immune systems. Nevertheless, Jesus questions any linear rewards-punishments approach to sickness and health, and poverty and success.

> *God makes the sun rise upon the evil and the good, and sends rain on the righteous and unrighteous. — Matthew 5:45*
> *Or those eighteen who were killed when the Tower of Siloam fell on them – do you think they were worse offenders than those living in Jerusalem? — Luke 13:4*
> *In the case of the man born blind, Jesus responds: "Neither this man nor his parents sinned; he was born blind so that God's works might be revealed in him." — John 9:3*

Other Christians assert that God is the ultimate source of good and evil and health and illness. Everything in the universe from plane crashes to cancer reflects God's will. Traditionally this belief has been described by the word, "omnipotence." God has all the power, everything that happens occurs either by God's choice or permission. For Reformer John Calvin, everything from our eternal salvation to the falling of a leaf reflects God's will. From eternity God has chosen every event in your life to fulfill God's good pleasure and purpose in the universe. Our death is written in God's book long before we are born. In its most extreme form, Calvin and his followers asserted that salvation and damnation are entirely God's doing and have nothing to do with our efforts. Whatever God wills is good regardless of its consequences for our present life or eternal destiny. While this exalts God's grace in the lives of the blessed and chosen, making it entirely unconditional and delivering us from the bondage of working out our salvation on our own, it also makes God the source of evil as well as good. God determines how long I will live, whether I accept Jesus as my savior, or if I will sail through life unscathed, dying quietly in my bed, or die in agony from ALS (Lou Gehrig's disease) or incurable cancer. If I am paralyzed in a car accident, it is God's doing; if I win the lottery, and enjoy a life of leisure it is God's doing. If I'm born blind, it is God's doing. For those persons living on the sunny side of life, God is good all the time. But, for those stricken with illness and poverty, God is fierce in God's apparently unjust, immutable, and arbitrary persecution.

A modern version of Calvin's theology comes from popular pastor Rick Warren. Warren does not advocate double predestination – the doctrine that God chooses both saved and damned – but he sees God as the source of every important event in our lives. According to Warren, God's "purpose for your life predates your conception. He planned it before you existed, *without your input.*"[1] Warren continues, "God prescribed every detail of your body. He deliberately chose your race, the color of your skin, your hair, and every other feature. He custom-made your body just the way he wanted it. He also determined the natural talents you would possess and the uniqueness of your personality."[2] Warren states God even chose your parents; it doesn't matter whether they were good or bad, for God's purpose is being fulfilled in their parenting. When we argue that our pain is needless and that our lives would have been more fulfilling if our parents had not abused us, Warren counters our complaints with the statement that "God has a pur-

1 Rick Warren, *The Purpose Driven Life* (Grand Rapids, MI: Zondervan, 2002), 21.
2 Ibid., 22-23.

pose behind every problem. Regardless of the cause, none of your problems could have occurred without God's permission. Everything that happens in your life is *Father-filtered* and he intends to use it for good."[1]

Much of what happens to us, Warren asserts, is a test in order for God to observe how we'll respond. Yet, Warren's clear affirmation of divine providence as shaping people in the same way that a potter forms clay, begs a number of questions: What happens to those who fail the tests of life? Are they rejected by the One who set unreasonable demands for them? Further, is the incurable cancer of a five year old "father filtered" or was God "testing" the people of Haiti, the children of those who died in the 9/11 attacks, or a child born with fetal alcohol syndrome as a result of her mother's substance abuse?

The philosopher Friedrich Nietzsche once said that "whatever doesn't kill me makes me stronger." While we certainly can grow in response to life's challenges, is the growth we experience sufficient justification for the pain we and those around us have to endure? When Jesus described his mission with these words, "I have come that they might have life, and have it abundantly" (John 10:10), he surely wasn't describing a God whose love hurts as well as heals, and who sends tsunamis to punish, educate, or test humankind.

Puzzling Passages. Both of the passages from John's Gospel can lead to confusion and suggest that our suffering is caused by God either to promote God's glory or punish us for our sin. A closer look, however, opens up the possibility of alternative, life-giving readings of these passages.

John 5:1-18 describes Jesus' encounter with a man who had sat at healing shrine for thirty-eight years. Jesus picks him out from the crowd and asks him a pointed, yet potential life-transforming question, "Do you want to be made well?" While his response ought to be an obvious affirmation and request for a cure, the man gives the reasons – or the excuses – why he has not been healed in the past. His reasoning is accurate – "Sir, I have no one to put me

---

1 Ibid., 194.

in the pool when the water is stirred up and when I am making my way, someone else steps down ahead of me." But, this isn't what Jesus is asking. Jesus is aiming the man toward the future by asking him to declare what he wants out of life. He is asking him to share his hopes and dreams, and in so doing, awaken the possibility for God's healing power to change his life.

Sensing the man's passivity, Jesus calls him to be an agent in his own healing. "Stand up, take your mat, and walk." Presented with a choice, the man for once takes a chance and chooses to be well. Yet, his healing provokes controversy and a further insight into his character. As he walks toward home, he is accosted by certain orthodox leaders who remind him that carrying his mat on the Sabbath is unlawful. Rather than claiming his agency in the matter, either by dropping the mat or continuing on his way home with mat in hand, the man once again succumbs to passivity. He blames Jesus for his infraction of religious law: "The man who made me well said to me, 'take up your mat and walk.'"

In light of his passivity, Jesus' words become a challenge to personal responsibility rather than an expression of divine punishment. "See, you have been made well. Do not sin anymore, so that nothing worse happens to you." Jesus is challenging the man to claim his agency and partnership with God in the healing process. Persons in Twelve Step groups affirm the importance of their healing – their recovery from addiction – one day at a time. Perhaps, passivity had gotten this man into trouble and stretched out the healing process into four decades. The healing he needed – encompassing mind, body, and spirit – might have been there all along. He might have been able to get up on his own or find a pathway to wholeness apart from the help of others or the angelic stirring of the waters.

Prone to let events determine his life, Jesus reminds him of the power of personal choice. We can choose our attitude and discover possibilities amid the limitations of life. When we become agents in our own lives, choosing partnership in God's healing adventures, we open up to new energies that can become tipping point between health and illness, and life and death. We are not all-powerful, nor can we create our own realities, but our decisions shape how we experience life and can lead to liberating hope and equanimity in the most challenging situations. In claiming our agency, we become actors in our own health and healing, rather than passive victims of our diagnosis and medical condition.

In Jesus' encounter with a man blind from birth, he makes it clear that this man's illness is not the result of sin or poor decision-making. He also suggests that his blindness is not entirely random, but may lead people to affirm God's presence and healing in the world. "He was born blind so that God's works might be revealed in the world." Now, this can be puzzling and troubling passage if we interpret it to mean that God caused a lifetime of blindness to reveal God's ultimate healing power. This man's suffering would be a means to an end, God's glory, and such behavior on the part of the Divine Parent would fall far short of any loving human parent.

The best of human parents recognize that struggle and effort are part of personal growth. As a grandparent of a toddler, I don't satisfy his every whim, nor do I step in to solve all of his problems. I let him fret a moment, then show him a way to solve the particular problem in front of him, whether it's retrieving a ball under the bookshelf or learning to climb up the steps. Still, I monitor his frustration level and intervene when he goes beyond his breaking point or might hurt himself. Perhaps, we can understand Jesus' intent in light of two correct, but differently nuanced, translations of Romans 8:28:

> *All things work together for good for those who love God*
> *or*
> *In all things God works for good.*

The first translation implies that God causes or makes all things occur by God's good pleasure, including negative events. The second translation suggests that God is not responsible for everything that occurs but that God works within human decisions, random events, and regular cause and effect relationships to bring about the best possible outcomes for us and the world. God seeks abundant life for all of us, but must work within human frailty and decision-making to achieve God's vision for our lives and the world.

Another Explanation. Perhaps, we will never solve the problem of pain as a theological issue. Pain can be life-changing for good or ill. Illness can remind us about what is important in life. We can find our treasure in following God's path and spending time with loved ones rather than workaholic behaviors. We can reach out to the least of these rather than focus on consumption and immediate gratification. I truly believe that God is at work in our vulnerability, but God's goal is for us to grow in grace and abundant life in every situation. God wants us to grow in wisdom and stature, even in the hospice setting or the graveside. The evidence of Jesus' ministry points to a God who seeks health, wholeness, and abundant life. Jesus surely affirmed the words of Jeremiah: "For surely I know the plans for you, says the Lord, plans for your welfare and not your harm, to give you future with hope" (Jeremiah 29:11).

I believe that health and illness are many-faceted in nature. Our well-being depends on a variety of interdependent and dynamic factors, including: the quality of the environment, the impact of our family origin, economic issues, our communities, our places of employment, along with our spiritual lives, the prayers of others, and God's quest for healing for us and all creation. I believe that God intimately and personally works within the events of our lives to bring about the best possible outcomes, often in situations that God has not chosen and must fight against along with our physicians, prayer partners, and ourselves. In this context our prayers, the prayers of others, and God's movements within the world can be the "tipping point" between health and illness, recovery and death. While there may be certain situations that appear to be outside our control as well as God's will – for example, incurable cancer – God is still working to promote healing even if a cure cannot be found. As many of us can affirm with the Apostle Paul, within vulnerability and weakness we can find strength, hope, and purpose. When there cannot be a cure there can always be a healing.

The multi-faceted nature of health and well-being provides a context for Jesus' final comment to the blind man prior to placing a healing poultice on his eyes. "We must work the works of God who sent me while it is day, night is coming when no one can work." In other words, the ultimate solution to the problem of pain is God's involvement in our lives and our willingness to take on the pain of others in healing ways. Our vocation as God's followers is to be healers wherever we are, blessing everyone we meet in Jesus' name, and providing the physical, economic, and spiritual support vulnerable persons need.

German theologian Dietrich Bonhoeffer stated that only a suffering God can save. Anglo-American philosopher Alfred North Whitehead asserted that God is the fellow sufferer who understands. God is right here where the pain is, moving within every cell and each soul to elicit the healing that is needed in this time and place. Innovative, imaginative, and energetic, God invites healing companions – physicians, nurses, pastors, prayer partners, complementary healers – to help tip the balance toward wholeness of mind, body, spirit, and relationships. Despite our prayers and healing practices, there are no guarantees of a cure, but God is with us feeling our pain and inspiring us to be agents of healing in our world.

HEALING MARKS

In this time of reflection, take time to reflect on the words of Psalm 46:10, written in a time of chaos and challenge, "be still and know that I am God." Remember also the words that Jesus spoke to his disciples on the evening of his resurrection: "Peace be with you. As the Father has sent me, so I send you." When he said this, he breathed on them and said, "Receive the Holy Spirit" (John 20:22). Every breath can be a healing breath, a calming breath, and an inspiring breath.

Take some time to find a comfortable position. Simply notice your breath, the most basic and in many ways the most important element of your life. Breathe gently, inhaling and exhaling, with the intention to open to God's Spirit with every breath. After several minutes, enter a state of prayerful awareness, pondering the question "Do you want to be made well?" Where are you in need of healing? What are you willing to do – honestly – to experience the healing you need? Let any images come to the surface without censorship. Perhaps the answer will come today, or at a later time. You may choose to ask the question more than once, with the recognition that we need healing at many layers.

After a time of reflection and prayer, again open to God's Wisdom, with the question, "To whom am I called to share God's healing presence? In what ways can I be God's healing partner in her or his life?" Listen for God's whispers in your breath and thoughts. Take time to pray for the person whose image or name emerges.

Conclude by asking for God's blessing on yourself and the one to whom you are called to share God's healing presence, asking for wisdom in becoming a channel of God's healing touch.

CHAPTER FOUR

FORGIVENESS AND HEALING

When he returned to Capernaum after some days, it was reported that he was at home. ²So many gathered around that there was no longer room for them, not even in front of the door; and he was speaking the word to them. ³Then some people came, bringing to him a paralyzed man, carried by four of them. ⁴And when they could not bring him to Jesus because of the crowd, they removed the roof above him; and after having dug through it, they let down the mat on which the paralytic lay. ⁵When Jesus saw their faith, he said to the paralytic, "Son, your sins are forgiven." ⁶Now some of the scribes were sitting there, questioning in their hearts, ⁷"Why does this fellow speak in this way? It is blasphemy! Who can forgive sins but God alone?" ⁸At once Jesus perceived in his spirit that they were discussing these questions among themselves; and he said to them, "Why do you raise such questions in your hearts? ⁹Which is easier, to say to the paralytic, 'Your sins are forgiven,' or to say, 'Stand up and take your mat and walk'? ¹⁰But so that you may know that the Son of Man has authority on earth to forgive sins" —he said to the paralytic— ¹¹"I say to you, stand up, take your mat and go to your home." ¹²And he stood up, and immediately took the mat and went out before all of them; so that they were all amazed and glorified God, saying, "We have never seen anything like this!" – Mark 2:1-12

The Molecules of Emotion. Medicine has rediscovered the whole person. Liberated from its bondage to Rene Descartes' mind-body dualism, contemporary medicine is realizing that mind and body constantly shape one another. The mind is embodied, and the body is constantly inspired, in the intricate and intimate connection of souls and cells. Chemical imbalances can lead to depression, anxiety, and bi-polar disorders. Conversely, emotional states – stress, grief, fear, guilt, anger – have been found to influence physical well-being. Some physicians note that stress-related issues, including issues of guilt and alienation, are a factor in the majority of physician visits. Dr. David Levy asserts that medical research along with his work with patients indicate that "emotions affect the immune system, for better or worse. Happiness heals like a medicine. Bitterness kills like a disease."[1]

The placebo and nocebo effects demonstrate that our beliefs can influence biology. Our positive and negative beliefs and expectations can influence how we feel. In medicine placebos, or non-medical treatments, are often employed to evaluate medical remedies. Patients taking placebos often experience similar benefits (for example, pain relief) as well as similar negative side effects as medical treatments. When people are given "nocebos," negative messages about a medication or food, they often exhibit negative physical symptoms. More recently, both the "relaxation response," evoked through the practice of meditation, and biofeedback demonstrate the power of the mind to influence overall well-being. Meditative states reduce blood pressure and stress, while biofeedback exercises can help people reduce the symptoms of stress, migraine headaches, and high blood pressure. The word reflected in our attitudes and emotional life is always made flesh in our immune, circulatory, digestive, and nervous system.

In biofeedback, the clinician uses precise instruments to measure physiological activity such as brainwaves, heart function, breathing, muscle activity, and skin temperature, which immediately "feedback" information to the patient. The presentation of this information – joined with changes in thinking, emotions, and behavior – often produces positive physiological changes which can be maintained outside the clinical setting. Research proves what the ancients knew intuitively – mind and body are connected and if you experience spiritual healing or positively alter your response to

---

1 David Levy, *Gray Matter: A Neurosurgeon Discovers the Power of Prayer...One Patient at a Time* (Carol Stream, IL, 2011) 132.

a certain situation, it will be reflected in greater physical well-being. While we are not omnipotent in shaping our health and well-being, we are not passive victims of our health condition whether we are facing cancer, heart disease, or the impact of emotional states like guilt and alienation. As Jesus said, "your faith has made you well" (Mark 5:34). And, as the apostle Paul echoed, you can be transformed "by the renewing of your mind" (Romans 12:2). We can just as easily affirm, with physician David Levy, that "forgiveness has well-documented health benefits."[1] Conversely, alienation, guilt, and inability to forgive can be factors in illness.

Darrell knows the power of emotions to shape physical well-being. Fearful of his employer's authoritarian style, he shook whenever he thought about his abusive treatment of his employees. His work-related stress was manifest in high blood pressure, insomnia, and constant fatigue and susceptibility to colds. Although he treated his ailments with medication, Darrell wanted to become free of the fear that imprisoned him. In Darrell's own words, "it was a matter of fight or flight. I could have stayed around and confronted the boss, but at the time I didn't have the guts. I began looking for a new job and found a position with a more positive supervisor. But, I realized my emotional work wasn't finished. There's always conflict in the workplace and I didn't want it to ruin my health. I didn't want old personal scripts to undermine my new position. I decided to seek out a Christian therapist who invited me to share about my fear of conflict and overbearing authority figures, beginning with my emotionally abusive father. He also taught me how to meditate and exercise to reduce my stress. I feel renewed and healed now that I have the ability to respond creatively to stress and conflict."

Allison felt tremendous guilt after her father died. She realized that she had not been the daughter he'd hoped for. This placed a wedge between them – Allison never felt she measured up to his expectations, so she chose to avoid him except on special occasions. Sadly, he berated her for her lack of personal attention and career

---

1 Ibid., 12.

and relational choices. When her father died, Allison was away on business and never had a chance to say goodbye or reconcile with her father. Feelings of bitterness and guilt plagued her and showed up in an inability to focus on her work, emotional distance from her family, and constant sense of fatigue. In describing her feelings, Allison notes, "I was heart-broken because we never overcame our alienation. I wished we'd reconciled. I know I needed to forgive him to move ahead in life, and he needed to forgive me for not being the person he wanted me to be. I have no regrets about my career or marriage, but the guilt I felt was tearing me apart emotionally and physically. I knew that I needed an emotional healing. I went to my pastor, who reminded me that all of us have sinned and fallen short of God's plan for our lives. She also told me that I could experience God's forgiveness and reconcile with my father."

Allison and her pastor met for several weeks for conversation and prayer. Each time her pastor prayed for a healing of the spirit as she laid hands upon Allison. Allison's healing was not immediate, but over time, she began to accept God's forgiveness and forgive her father. Allison's pastor invited her to visualize herself in a conversation in the company of both her father and Jesus. As Allison recalls, "I was initially afraid to confront my father even in my imagination. But, when I found that Jesus was with both of us, and that he would protect me from any verbal abuse I might receive, I felt the courage to share how I felt and to say 'I love you' to my Dad. For the first time, I saw my dad as he was – not all-powerful or all-wise, but just a guy who hoped, and thought he knew best in insuring that his daughter would have a good life and failed miserably in sharing his love for her. I realize now that he regretted the distance between us, but couldn't change his behavior any more than I could change my fear of him. Now I know he loved me, but – like me – he just couldn't reach out and bury the hatchet. We ended up in a group hug with Jesus." Her reconciliation with her father was not the end of the story. Allison has regained her focus, energy, and emotional transparency. While she's no hurry to get to heaven, Allison now has hope, as she says, that "I can get to know

my Dad in heaven. We can have the relationship I always wanted."
Whenever negative memories return, Allison returns to her place
of safety with Jesus shielding her from any harm she fears from her
father. In fact, these days she is rediscovering positive memories of
her relationship with her father.

Breakthrough to Healing. When we make a commitment
to the healing journey, we discover that new possibilities and energies open up for us. The world becomes a place of synchronous
encounters, insights, and answers to prayer. We also discover the
roadblocks that stand in our way. Sometimes things about which
we were oblivious become boulders that block our pathway to
the future – socially-acceptable addictions, negative self-talk, low
self-esteem, alienation, anxiety, and the impact of social stereotypes
regarding age, gender, and education. There are times that we are
tempted to live with the status quo and accept the fact that we
will just have to live with our physical, emotional, relational, and
spiritual pain and dysfunctionality. But, the boulders can become
angels, that is, messengers of God and inspirations to courage and
growth when we step out on faith. Faith doesn't guarantee an easy
path or success, but it places us in companionship with the living
and healing God, whose vision for us is healing and wholeness,
whether or not a cure can be achieved.

Like virtually every healing story, we just get a snapshot of
what really happened. Put simply, a man is paralyzed, unable to
navigate on his own. The word spreads that the healer is in town.
His friends are inspired to take to him to Jesus to secure the physical
healing that he needs. The language of the story – "when Jesus saw
their faith" – is ambiguous: does it refer just to the four friends or
does it include the man stricken with paralysis? In any event, the
friends' faith is crucial to the recovery of their paralyzed friend.
Without their loyalty and persistence he would never have experienced a cure.

Drama and decision characterize this story. When the four
men arrive at Jesus' home, carrying their friend, the crowds are so
great that they cannot gain entry and are faced with a moment of

decision. Perhaps, their friend – who might have come grudgingly
to begin with – wants to give up. He may have muttered "I knew
that this was a fool's errand. Let's just go home. There's nothing
we can do." But, the friends are undeterred. I imagine that they
surveyed the grounds, saw the stairway leading to the rooftop and,
despite their friend's protests, carefully mounted the stairs, and began the work of dismantling the straw roof. They took a risk legally
and relationally. They were destroying private property and, if they
were arrested or failed in their quest for a healing, they would be
the objects of ridicule throughout the community.

Love guides them up the roof top. In fact, it may be love – just
as much as faith in Jesus – that enables them to become partners
in God's healing adventure.

Their story invites us to explore the obstacles that stand in the
way of our healing and the healing of those we love. It also invites us
to challenge our own complacency regarding social conditions that
contribute to illness, such as lack of education, poverty, inability to
navigate the health care system, and privately-rationed health care.
After all, healing involves prevention as much as treatment and
addressing the social causes of illness as much as providing medical
responses to what could have been prevented by better housing,
diet, and domestic security. This healing story challenges us to
consider: What boulders – individually, socially, and politically - do
we need to challenge in our quest to become God's companions in
healing the world and those we love?

Mark recognizes that obstacles often accompany our quest for
healing and wholeness. The healings of Jairus' daughter, the woman
with the flow of blood, blind Bartimaeus, and the Syrophoenecian
woman's daughter were initially met with resistance, either from
naysayers, social and religious mores, or ethnic divisions. Yet, they
persisted and their persistence opened the door to a healing burst
of divine energy.

The friends succeed in breaking through the roof, and are met
by Jesus' caring gaze. Others might have seen their presence as an
intrusion or an annoyance, a violation of the decency and order

that is required in spiritual settings. But, Jesus saw their courage and faith as an opportunity for a healing that encompassed body, mind, spirit, and relationships. As the scripture says: "When Jesus saw their faith, he said to the paralytic, 'Son, your sins are forgiven.'"

These surprising words of forgiveness ignited a controversy between Jesus and the religious teachers. Jesus may have seen something that everyone – including the paralyzed man – had overlooked. His paralysis might have been spiritual and emotional as well as physical. The cause of his physical disability may have been a deep-seated psychological wound or an action he had committed long ago, perhaps, unknown to others that led to disabling feelings of guilt. Jesus may also have been challenging the social and religious context which identified sickness and sin. The man's paralysis may have been purely physical in origin, but that did not stop the local moralists from judging him as a sinner, beyond the care of a righteous God. Whatever the case, this man needed a complete healing, encompassing every aspect of his life, to stand up and walk again.

Cells and Souls. Jesus truly was a holistic healer. He recognized the intimate interconnectedness of mind, body, and spirit. He was well aware of the negative impact of theological and social stigmas that rendered diseased and disabled persons unclean in the eyes of religious and social leaders. Blaming the victim twice – for her sins and for her illness – compounds the suffering vulnerable people experience. Jesus also knew that spiritual and emotional healing was as difficult as physical cures. Listen to Jesus' words to those who challenge his right to forgive sins:

> *Which is easier, to say to the paralytic, 'Your sins are forgiven,' or to say, 'Stand up and take your mat and walk'?* [10]*But so that you may know that the Son of Man has authority on earth to forgive sins"* —*he said to the paralytic*— [11]*"I say to you, stand up, take your mat and go to your home."* [12]*And he stood up, and immediately took the mat and went out before all of them.– Mark 2:9-12*

Could this man have been a victim of his own guilt or inability to forgive? According to physician David Levy: "Many people suffer physical problems because of what happened to them in the past.... They are unable or unwilling to forgive someone who hurt them, and a couple things happen. It drives them away from God and becomes a poison in their physical bodies that crops up in all sorts of problems.... Sometimes they have headaches, sometimes they can't sleep, and sometimes their immune systems get so compromised that their diseases get the upper hand on them."[1]

There are two poles of forgiveness – accepting forgiveness when you have harmed others and the act of forgiving those whom we perceive have harmed us. Jesus connects the two: even the blameless need to let go of the burden of their inability to forgive. In the words of the Lord's prayer, "Forgive us our debts as we also have forgiven our debtors" (Matthew 6:12). To experience healing, the elder brother, described in the Parable of the Prodigal Son, must let go of his feelings of self-righteousness and moral superiority, embrace his wayward brother, and join the party. Otherwise, his alienation will poison his relationships and may surface in stress-related illness or a compromised immune system.

Forgiveness was no academic exercise for the healer Jesus. On the cross, he asked that God forgive his tormentors: "Father, forgive them, for they know not what they do" (Luke 23:34).

Bearing grudges alienates and creates disharmony that poisons relationships and may very well, due to the stress of anger, threaten our physical well-being. When we forgive, two people receive God's healing touch: the one we've forgiven and ourselves.

The story is told of a politician who asked President Abraham Lincoln how he would treat the rebellious Southerners after the war. The questioner expected words of vengeance and acts of violence. He was astounded when Lincoln replied, "I would treat them as if they had never left." Hatred, recriminations, blaming, and grudge-keeping only lead to more violence and hatred. Only the peace that surpasses understanding, the amazing grace of forgive-

---

1 David Levy, *Gray Matter*, 264.

ness, can heal our spirits and restore fellowship with God, ourselves, and our enemies.

Elizabeth Kübler Ross once responded to the book, *I'm OK, You're OK,* with the words, "I'm not ok, and you're not ok, but it's ok." This is the meaning of grace and the power of forgiveness to transform cells and spirits. Asking for and accepting forgiveness can change our lives. Grace abounds, but we can block God's amazing grace, by failing to recognize that we need it. Like many evangelical children, I grew up going to Billy Graham crusades and watching the "Hour of Decision" on television. Each sermon ended with an altar call and the singing of "Just as I am." Whether we identify ourselves as evangelical, conservative, progressive, or agnostic, these words speak to our need for forgiveness and the power of forgiveness to release us from the deadening power of spiritual, emotional, physical, and relational burdens.

> Just as I am, without one plea,
> but that thy blood was shed for me,
> and that thou bidst me come to thee,
> O Lamb of God, I come, I come.
>
> Just as I am, though tossed about
> with many a conflict, many a doubt,
> fightings and fears within, without,
> O Lamb of God, I come, I come.
>
> Just as I am, poor, wretched, blind;
> sight, riches, healing of the mind,
> yea, all I need in thee to find,
> O Lamb of God, I come, I come.
>
> Just as I am, thou wilt receive,
> wilt welcome, pardon, cleanse, relieve;
> because thy promise I believe,
> O Lamb of God, I come, I come. [1]

---

1 Charlotte Elliot, "Just as I Am," (1835), verses 1, 3, 4, 5

Centuries earlier, the Epistle of James affirmed the unity of body, mind, and spirit in the healing process.

> *Are any among you sick? They should call for the elders of the church and have them pray over them, anointing them with oil in the name of the Lord. *[15]*The prayer of faith will save the sick, and the Lord will raise them up; and anyone who has committed sins will be forgiven. *[16]*Therefore confess your sins to one another, and pray for one another, so that you may be healed. The prayer of the righteous is powerful and effective. – James 5:14-16*

We don't know the inner life of this paralyzed man, but the story suggests that Jesus addressed both his physical and spiritual needs. Like the healing of Jairus' daughter, the healing of the paralyzed man was a communal healing resulting from the faith of friends, the willingness of the man (even with all his reservations) to come to Jesus, and Jesus' ability to liberate bodies and spirits. Though apparently passive, the paralyzed man becomes an agent in his own healing process. Following Jesus' command, he stands up, picks up the mat, and walks. He stands up, first, on the inside by accepting Jesus' forgiveness and taking the chance that he might stumble and fall, and be publically humiliated once more. His inner healing is mirrored by his outer action. He becomes a partner with his friends and Jesus in the dynamic call and response of grace and forgiveness, and invitation and action. Healing always expands our freedom and creativity and deepens our ability to enter into relationship with God and our fellow humans.

This healing story is a call to forgiveness and confession, whether we are physically healthy or experiencing debilitating illness. It is not ultimately about guilt, but letting go of guilt and letting God heal your life. It invites us to trust God fully with our past and the limits that have emerged from decisions that have harmed us and others. It invites us to let go of perfectionism and unnecessary guilt for things that are out of our control or for which we were not responsible. It challenges us to recognize our fallibility and, in so doing, forgive universally and completely, even when we have to let issues related to the justice system take their course in the lives of those who have broken the law, harming us or others. After confessing your feelings of guilt, anger, and personal fallibilities to God or to a spiritual friend, who mediates God's love to you, your life may not immediately change and you still may face the temptation to return to negative behaviors and harmful habits, but your spirit will be lighter and your step more energetic, for now you know that you are forgiven, accepted, and loved.

HEALING MARKS

One of my favorite stories involves Michelangelo, a neighbor, and a boulder. One day, a neighbor observed the sculptor rolling a boulder up the hill to his front porch. The sculptor took out his chisel and began pounding on the boulder. Overcome by curiosity, the neighbor crossed the street and asked the Michelangelo, "Why are you hammering on that boulder?" To which Michelangelo responded, "There's an angel inside and I'm trying to let it out."

In a God-inspired universe, there are angels – messengers, inspirations, and energies – within every boulder that stands in our way. In this time of spiritual examination, I invite you to take some time for quiet introspection, either in a comfortable chair or as you go for a walk. Consider the boulders – emotional, spiritual, physical, and relational – that have stood in the way of your embodiment of God's vision for your life and well-being. What are these boulders? Insofar as you can discern their source, how did they come into your life? In what ways, if any, are they a result of your decisions, attitudes, or values? How would your life be different if you could bring forth angels from these boulders?

As you contemplate these boulders, enter into a time of prayer. Ask God to reveal to you how you can move these boulders out of your path. Do you need to be forgiven? Is there anyone you need to forgive? Take time to experience forgiveness and forgive others, remembering that God is ready to heal us long before we think we need healing.

If possible, visualize the angels emerging from these boulders. What gifts of personal growth and well-being do they have for you? Visualize yourself as healed, whole, forgiving, and forgiven.

Conclude by thanking God for the healing power of forgiveness and the gift of new and abundant life.

CHAPTER FIVE

THE HEALING OF PURPOSE[1]

Jesus went out again beside the lake; the whole crowd gath-
ered around him, and he taught them. [14]As he was walking along,
he saw Levi son of Alphaeus sitting at the tax booth, and he said
to him, 'Follow me.' And he got up and followed him.
    [15]And as he sat at dinner in Levi's house, many tax-collectors
and sinners were also sitting with Jesus and his disciples—for there
were many who followed him. [16]When the scribes of the Pharisees
saw that he was eating with sinners and tax-collectors, they said
to his disciples, 'Why does he eat with tax-collectors and sinners?'
[17]When Jesus heard this, he said to them, 'Those who are well have
no need of a physician, but those who are sick; I have come to call
not the righteous but sinners.' – Mark 2:13-17

Vocational Healing. Jesus' approach to healing was both universal and intimate. Healing involved more than the restoration
of physical well-being, also involved social standing, emotional
life, spirituality, and sense of purpose and vocation. It embraced
the lives of communities as well as individuals in Jesus' quest to
embody God's realm of Shalom "on earth as it is in heaven" (Matthew 6:10). Everyone is in need of God's healing touch to achieve
her or his personal fulfillment, true happiness, and place in God's
vision for the world.

    The call of Levi is seldom categorized as a healing story. But,
in reality, few things are more important or more challenging than
finding our personal calling or vocation. Frederick Buechner has
noted that "the place God calls you to is the place where your

---

1 This chapter title is taken from John Biersdof's insightful book, *The
Healing of Purpose* (Nashville: Abingdon, 1985).

deep gladness and the world's deep hunger meet."[1] I would add that a person's calling is the intersection of her or his gifts and the world's needs. Many persons wander about aimlessly, looking for fulfillment in all the wrong places, until they pause long enough to hear God's still small voice, whispering within the many voices competing for their attention and allegiance. God calls to us with possibilities each moment, throughout the day, and over the course of a lifetime. With Esther, God always calls us "for just a time as this," and God also calls us in the gifts and talents around which we can orient our life's vocation.

We don't know much about Levi, but we can imaginatively re-construct the story of his call to discipleship. He was a tax collector, whose place of business resembled a contemporary toll booth or air-port security station. To travel on the toll road, a pilgrim, family, or merchant would have present documents and pay a fee. Like today's Internal Revenue Service in some peoples' minds, persons in Levi's position represented power, authority, and intimidation. They were employees of the much hated and feared Roman oppressor. Every-one knew the scam. Tax collectors worked on a commission basis, that is, they had to turn over a certain sum of money to the local Roman authorities; their own salary came from what they earned above and beyond the basic surcharges. They set the fees and put the difference in their pockets. Tax collectors lived well, but found themselves in a financial and social vice grip. They had to please the Romans who looked at them solely as a source of income, set fees according their arbitrary standards, and saw them as functionaries. Despite the financial benefits the occupying forces accrued from their employment, their Roman employers looked down upon them as traitors to their own people. Moreover, their fellow citizens treated them with contempt, viewing them as traitors and religious outcasts, unclean by their association with Gentile pigs! Unable to participate in Jewish society and religion, and looked down upon

---

1 http://www.pbs.org/wnet/religionandethics/week936/interview.html. Last accessed October 29, 2012.

by their employers, their only companions were fellow outcasts – upper middle class income, but social pariahs.

We don't know much more about Levi than his occupation and social standing as an affluent outcast and sinner. But, we imagine that if he had a sensitive conscience, he may have felt a profound unrest and sense of captivity. He could never escape the impact of his occupation – religiously, socially, or interpersonally. He might have been born into outsider status, and inherited his father's occupation because it was the only one for which he was qualified as a religious and social sinner. I suspect that Levi had not only heard about Jesus but had interacted with him in the course of his daily occupation. He might have charged Jesus and his followers tolls for using the Roman road, and in the course of their interactions, Jesus might have surprised him by treating him with generous hospitality as an equal, neither fearing nor scorning him, but approaching him with care and affirmation. Jesus may even have shared his vision that God's good news included tax collectors like Levi.

I suspect that something deep within Levi's spirit cried out for new life. He had overheard Jesus' call to a new self and to new spiritual values, and when Jesus asked him to follow, he took the first steps on a holy adventure that would lead through conflict, surprise, transformation, and personal fulfillment. Levi had met the Physician of the Spirit and experienced a healing of purpose and vocation. He had found his deepest calling as a follower of the Teacher and Healer, whose realm embraced "sinners," people whose occupations, ethnicity, and health condition, rendered them religiously unclean, and invited them to be full-fledged members of God's healing realm.

From Waywardness to Vocation. A person doesn't need to be a religious outcast, morally challenged, or physically or mentally ill to need a healing of purpose and vocation. Many of us are doing all the "right things" in terms of our culture, profession, and social context, but still feel restless, unfulfilled, and lacking in purpose or vision. We may be successful and affluent, the envy of others, and feel directionless, living what nineteenth century philosopher

Henry David Thoreau described as a life of quiet desperation. Like Ivan Illych, the protagonist of Leo Tolstoy's novel, we may discover that as we rise professionally, we are drifting further from our calling in life. Often an illness calls us back to what's important in life and challenges us to discover a reason to live and a hope for tomorrow. Personal experience suggests that discovering our calling in life may be reflected in our overall well-being, quality of life, and life expectancy. A restoration of hope and vision can transform our spirits and restore our immune systems.

Although she was a successful attorney, Diane felt something was missing in her life. She had a lovely Manhattan townhouse, skied in Vermont, and dressed in the latest fashions. Everything changed with the diagnosis of cancer. One Sunday, following her diagnosis, she heard her pastor read "what will it profit a person if she gains the world and loses her soul" (Mark 8:36). She heard an inner voice reminding her that "Life is more important than an apartment with a view and a prestigious position." She began to see a spiritual director along with a therapist and, for the first time in her adult life, began to question her personal and professional choices. Her illness called her to examine her spiritual life. She learned to meditate and visualize healing light entering her body along with the chemotherapy. It was a long process that included a sabbatical from work. But, as Diane began to feel better, she also began to explore new possibilities for her future. She discovered that while law was still her professional calling, she needed to change her orientation from corporate to environmental law. "I used to see my goal as making money and winning cases, now my vocation is to help save the earth. I've had to downsize, sell my apartment, and simplify my life, but I've never been happier. I believe I'm where God wants me to be." Diane is embodying the spirit of the Shaker hymn, "Simple Gifts" in her quest for God's partner in the quest for ecological justice:

> 'Tis the gift to be simple, 'tis the gift to be free
> 'Tis the gift to come down where we ought to be,

And when we find ourselves in the place just right,
'Twill be in the valley of love and delight.

When true simplicity is gain'd,
To bow and to bend we shan't be asham'd,
To turn, turn will be our delight,
Till by turning, turning we come 'round right.[1]

Diane has come round right. Her story is mirrored throughout scripture and daily life.

Discovering God's vision awakens undreamed of possibilities and unleashes unexpected energies for personal and global transformation. Sometimes, like Queen Esther you don't have to change your profession, but your attitude toward your position and the social responsibilities that go with it. When Mordecai challenged Esther to use her power for good – to save her people – she discovered that she had been raised to power for "just such a time as this" (Esther 4:14). She courageously came out of the closet as a Hebrew to alert the King to threats on her life and the well-being of her people.

Mary and Joseph discovered God's calling for their lives when they embraced the impossible possibility that they share in God's healing revelation to humankind. The Magi followed a star that took them beyond their homeland in search of the world's savior in a foreign land and among the people of a different faith tradition. Sometimes following God's vision for your life can bring you home by another route. You may need to change course and explore new territories – vocationally, spiritually, and professionally.

Twice in my life, I have been part of institutional downsizing: in both cases, I was forced to explore possibilities and embrace new visions for my future. Changing your spiritual or professional path is never easy. It wasn't easy for me, nor was it for Peter and the Zebedee brothers who left the family business to become pilgrims

---

1 Elder Joseph Brackett, "Simple Gifts" (1848).

of God's coming realm. But, when we discover that God is with us, giving us new possibilities along with new challenges, we face chosen and unexpected personal and professional changes with courage, hope, and ingenuity.

God's Healing Vision. God is both omnipresent and omni-active. God aims at abundant life in every situation, providing possibilities and the energy to receive them moment by moment and over a lifetime. There is a vocation for each moment of life, and there are long-term vocations that bring forth our gifts and lure them toward fulfillment. As Paul promised the Philippians, "The good work God has begun in your life God will bring to fulfillment ... and it will be a harvest of righteousness" (Philippians 1:3-11, sections). God's providence is never unilateral, nor does God – in contrast to Rick Warren's approach – determine all the important events of our lives without our input. Rather, God seeks to inspire our freedom and creativity to bring beauty, justice, and healing to our lives and the world. Whether it relates to our vocation or physical condition, the healing process is the result of the interplay of God's call and our response. Grace enhances rather than limits freedom. God wants us to be creative and adventurous; in freely exercising our freedom, we enable God to be more active in our lives, energizing body, mind, and spirit, and transforming our relationships.

HEALING MARKS

God calls us within the everyday tasks of our lives, infusing our lives with possibilities and the energy to achieve them. As Irenaeus of Lyon proclaims, the glory of God is a human being who is fully alive. To be fully alive is to experience divine healing, whether we are physically healthy, experiencing physical healing, or awaiting death. In this exercise, we will explore where your great joy and personal gifts respond to the needs of the world.

Begin by taking some time for quiet meditation, breathing deeply and experiencing yourself in the center of God's vision.

Visualize yourself in a place of peace and beauty. What is the environment like? What catches your eye? As you are enjoying the peaceful environment, you notice that Jesus is walking toward you. What does Jesus look like? As he stands beside you, he engages you in conversation. He asks you, "Where are you finding joy in your life?" How do you respond to his question? How does the conversation continue between Jesus and you? In the course of your conversation, Jesus asks, "Where is your passion in life? What possibilities lie ahead for you?" How do you respond?

Inspired by Jesus' words, visualize yourself moving toward the next steps in your calling. What is it like to embody God's vocation for your life? Experience yourself fulfilling God's vision for your life. Conclude by giving thanks for God's movements in your life and for the future possibilities that lie ahead for you.

In the week ahead, daily ask for God's guidance in finding your passion and embodying it in your vocational and personal life.

CHAPTER SIX

HEALING WITHOUT BOUNDARIES

From there he set out and went away to the region of Tyre. He entered a house and did not want anyone to know he was there. Yet he could not escape notice, ²⁵but a woman whose little daughter had an unclean spirit immediately heard about him, and she came and bowed down at his feet. ²⁶Now the woman was a Gentile, of Syrophoenician origin. She begged him to cast the demon out of her daughter. ²⁷He said to her, "Let the children be fed first, for it is not fair to take the children's food and throw it to the dogs." ²⁸But she answered him, "Sir, even the dogs under the table eat the children's crumbs." ²⁹Then he said to her, "For saying that, you may go—the demon has left your daughter." ³⁰So she went home, found the child lying on the bed, and the demon gone.

³¹Then he returned from the region of Tyre, and went by way of Sidon towards the Sea of Galilee, in the region of the Decapolis. ³²They brought to him a deaf man who had an impediment in his speech; and they begged him to lay his hand on him. ³³He took him aside in private, away from the crowd, and put his fingers into his ears, and he spat and touched his tongue. ³⁴Then looking up to heaven, he sighed and said to him, "Ephphatha," that is, "Be opened." ³⁵And immediately his ears were opened, his tongue was released, and he spoke plainly. ³⁶Then Jesus ordered them to tell no one; but the more he ordered them, the more zealously they proclaimed it. ³⁷They were astounded beyond measure, saying, "He has done everything well; he even makes the deaf to hear and the mute to speak." – Mark 7:24-37

An Unhindered Gospel in a World of Divisions. Just over fifty years ago, in the United States, bathrooms, swimming pools, hotels, lunch counters, and drinking fountains were labeled "whites only" and "colored only." Accidents of birth can lead to antipathy, exclusion, violence, and genocide. African-American theologian and pastor Howard Thurman tells the story of how playing with a neighborhood child awakened him to the traumatic nature of racism. The young girl he was playing with began to pinch and punch him as part of their game. Much to her surprise, he cried out in pain. She had been raised to believe that the children of slaves had the unique characteristic of being impervious to pain, a holdover from the days in which African Americans were believed to be little more than animals, unfeeling and unable to govern themselves rationally.

Historically humans have dehumanized and objectified other humans in order to abuse, kill, enslave, and imprison them. Even in the so-called enlightened second decade of the twenty-first century, we still hear racial epithets, ethnic slurs, sexist comments, and hate speech directed to gay, lesbian, bisexual, and transgender people. During the era of apartheid, Bishop Desmond Tutu referred to the South African policy of racial separation and oppression as a heresy, the denial of full humanity to God's beloved children, created in God's image. The words we use and the boundaries we create are not just political or verbal. They can contribute to self-limitation, low self-esteem, and hopelessness. Destroying the social fabric of a people of a community can be a factor in increased violence, substance abuse and can lead to the break-up of families and high incidence of absentee fathers and unwed mothers. God's dream of healing embraces communities as well as individuals. Following the prophetic vision of justice rolling like waters and righteousness, like an ever-flowing stream, Jesus' vision of abundant life led him to proclaim the reality of God's reign on earth:

> *The Spirit of the Lord is upon me,*
> *because he has anointed me*
> *to bring good news to the poor.*
> *He has sent me to proclaim release to the captives*
> *and recovery of sight to the blind,*

> *to let the oppressed go free,*
> *¹⁹ to proclaim the year of the Lord's favour. – Luke 4:18-19*

God's realm includes all people, nuisances and nobodies, un-clean women, generous Samaritans, tax collectors, and prostitutes. God's Spirit, as Peter proclaimed on Pentecost, is poured out upon "all flesh" and persons of every age, gender, or social condition. God's Shalom breaks down every barrier and heals every form of alienation and oppression.

A Scandalous Snapshot. Mark's Gospel is brutally honest about the spiritual maturity of the disciples, the reality of pain and suffering, and Jesus' own challenges. Mark is well aware of Jesus' finitude and the impact of the environment on Jesus' actions and ability to heal. Mark notes that Jesus' healing powers were limited because of the barriers of unbelief created in his hometown. Fur-ther, Mark recognizes that healing can be gradual and subtle as well as dramatic, when he describes a two-stage healing of sight im-paired man, hardly worthy of today's television healers. Moreover, in the words of one commentator, Mark describes Jesus caught with his compassion down in his encounter with this Syrophoenecian woman. The all-loving Jesus appears to be a racist in his response to this unnamed foreign woman.

As the parent of a child who was diagnosed with a life-threat-ening illness, I identify with the Syrophoenician woman's intensity and willingness to swallow her pride for her daughter's recovery. I would have done anything to insure my son's recovery. I would have endured the loss of an organ, humiliation, employment, and perhaps even death. I recall walking home with him one evening after a day of chemotherapy. Even though my son is four inches taller, and normally stronger, than I am, I was on alert ready to fight for his well-being as we walked through the urban neighborhood on our way from the hospital to his home.

In this healing account, an unnamed foreign woman comes to Jesus desperate for a cure. She has no doubt heard of his mag-ical powers to heal. Although she is from a different religion and ethnicity, she has nothing to lose by seeking out the healer. She comes to Jesus begging for a healing. Jesus appears to be off duty at the time and initially puts her off with an apparently racist remark, comparing her and her daughter to "dogs" unworthy of his healing touch. Undeterred, she humiliates herself, accepting Jesus' description of her as a dog, but making a claim the even dogs deserve consideration. The scraps at the table – just a small portion of Jesus' healing energy – are all her daughter needs to be delivered from the spirit that possessed her.

We don't know the nature of her daughter's ailment. In ancient and non-technological cultures, illness is often attributed to spirit possession. One ancient theory was that disease comes from the outside, the result of a malevolent spirit taking control of a person's body, mind, and spirit. Today, we might attribute her illness to a chemical or genetic disorder, a virus, or cellular aberration. Regardless of the cause, and we don't need to be limited by first century explanations of illness and its causes, parents are devastated when their children's well-being and safety is out of their control. In that momentary encounter, this foreign woman placed all her hopes in Jesus. You can imagine how shattered she felt when Jesus appeared to stand in the way of her daughter's recovery.

While we can't look into Jesus' heart to discover why he responded to this Gentile woman as he did, I believe that we can discern three possible reasons for his behavior. First, and least flattering, is that fatigued by the rigors of his ministry and taking a temporary sabbatical from the public eye, Jesus reverts to his people's default response to Gentiles – racial superiority, alienation, and objectification. As a member of God's chosen people, Jesus may have shared his fellow citizens' superior attitude toward unclean Gentiles. After all, first century Jewish males regularly thanked God that they were not females or Gentiles.

Second, Jesus may have been testing her faith, forcing her to declare the depth of her love of her daughter and how far she would go to secure her daughter's healing. As twelve step movements assert, "you've got to want it real bad!" Like the mother portrayed in the film *Lorenzo's Oil*, this woman will do anything, including opening herself to humiliation, for her daughter's well-being.

A final explanation is that this encounter is an embodied parable. Jesus appears to be racist, using the code language of ethnic superiority that sadly still persists among politicians and their followers, and his listeners nod their heads in agreement as he ratifies their feelings of superiority over the Gentile dogs. They no doubt chuckle and exchange knowing glances as he humiliates her. But, he pulls the rug out from under their racism by commending her faith and then pronouncing her daughter cured. The parable is enacted in Jesus' acceptance of her and his affirmation of her faith. Faithfulness to God can be found everywhere, including among those we disparage as a result of the accidents of birth.

We don't know what actually transpired in this curious and unflattering encounter, but Jesus who grew in wisdom and stature (Luke 2:52) may well have received a lesson in faith from this foreigner. She may have opened him to the Creator's care for all peoples and inspired him to expand his mission to the Gentile world.

As Jesus continues his journey toward the Sea of Galilee, he travels through the Decapolis, the "ten cities" where Gentiles were the majority people. He encounters a hearing and speech impaired man, whom he heals through a combination of prayer and spittle, spirituality and medicine. Could this man have been a Gentile, this time healed without commentary on Jesus' part, as a sign of God's ever-expanding realm of salvation (Mark 7:31-37)? Regardless of his ethnic background, Jesus prayerfully takes his condition to God and in the interplay of Jesus' love and God's presence, this man's speech and hearing is restored. Moreover, like the two other healings in Mark (the paralyzed man let down through the roof and Jairus' daughter), Jesus responds to the love of friends who bring him to the healer and takes him to a solitary place to make him whole.

Distant Healing. The universe we live in is profoundly dynamic and interdependent according to physicists, ecologists, and biologists. When the philosopher Alfred North Whitehead stated that the whole universe conspired to create each moment of experience, he was anticipating what has become orthodoxy among scientists, if not, pastors and politicians. Despite the rhetoric of some free market capitalists, there are no rugged individualists, nor can we separate mind, body, and emotions. We emerge from a lively universe of relationships that shape our experience and provide the materials for our own creativity.

Recently, scientists have been studying the sacred. Prayer and meditation have become objects of scientific research. Harvard Medical School professor Herbert Benson describes the impact of meditation on blood pressure and the immune system through his studies on the "relaxation response." Researcher Candace Pert speaks of the "molecules of emotion," the presence of emotional life in our stomachs as well as our brains. Physician Larry Dossey asserts that "prayer is good medicine" and cites a variety of studies that associate intercessory prayer with fewer side effects following surgery, the accelerated healing of wounds among mice and rats, and more rapid growth in experiments involving grass. Studies indicate that blessing our plants leads to greater growth, while cursing them impedes their flourishing.[1] Researchers are discovering the wisdom of my mother's refrigerator magnet, "prayer changes things." People of faith have always interceded on the behalf of others. While we cannot fully understand the mechanics of intercessory prayer, many of us pray for others on a daily basis, inspired by the faith that our prayers allow God to be more present and effective in transforming peoples' lives. I believe that our prayers radiate across the universe, unlimited by spatial separation or temporality. Our prayers can heal past memories, influence the future, and influence peoples' lives and situations in distant places.

The story of the Syrophoenecian woman is one of four distant healings, recorded in scripture. Matthew and Luke record the

---

1 For more on studies related to the impact of prayer and meditation on humans and non-humans, see the bibliographical selections at the end of the book.

healing of a Roman centurion's servant that cut across geography and ethnicity (Matthew 8:5-13, Luke 7:1-10). John's Gospel describes the distant healing of the son of a royal, probably Roman, official (John 4:46-54). Possibly, the accounts from Matthew, Luke, and John describe the same event and affirm Jesus' ability to transcend spatial limitations. In Jesus' ministry, there appears to be no distance in prayer, either temporally or geographically. Like the principles of contemporary physics, described by Bell's Theorem, two molecules that have at one time or another "touched" each other are able to mirror and influence each other's behavior across the universe.

Every morning as I take my sunrise walk, I offer intercessory prayers on behalf of my family, dearest friends, and people for whom I've been asked to pray. In the case of my son, daughter-in-law, grandson, and the second grandchild on the way, I pray for their well-being. In the case of a former student and my closest spiritual friend, both of whom are being treated for breast cancer, I boldly pray for a full recovery. I also pray for events in the future such as surgeries, job interviews, and talks and sermons.

I don't know the exact mechanics of intercessory prayer, but I have developed a flexible and tentative theology of intercessory prayer. In an interdependent and dynamic universe, I believe that prayer creates a positive field of force around those for whom we pray. It shapes their internal and external environment in ways that subtly influence their experience, hopes, possibilities, and dreams. It also creates an environment in which God can be more active in the healing process of mind, body, spirit, and relationships. I believe that the healing stories in Mark and the other gospels reveal a profound interdependence between our faith and God's action. God's call to healing is always prior to our response, but God's call is amplified by our ongoing commitment to the well-being of ourselves and others through lifestyle, attitude, and prayer. Our lack of faith can, as it did in Nazareth, block God's healing energies, but it cannot ultimately defeat them.

Prayer transcends the limits of time insofar as my prayers for healing of a past event can reduce or eliminate its impact on my present life. Whether we call this the healing of memories or the transformation of time, prayer changes the meaning of the past and liberates us from the burden of prior traumas, injustice, or pain. Moreover, when we pray for a future event, for example, tomorrow's surgery or a job interview, our prayers become part of the future we will experience, adding energy, insight, and openness to God in challenging situations.

Our prayers do not change God's intention for us and others. God's aim is always at abundant life, even for those who are competing for the same position or play on opposing teams. God's relationship to the world is never arbitrary or fickle, but always loving and supportive. Still, the nature of God's action in the world is always intimate and contextual. God always acts – even in ways that we perceive as miraculous – appropriate to every situation and person. Our prayers create an energetic openness at every level of life from cellular to spiritual through which God can act more decisively and inspirationally amid the many factors of life.

Prayer changes things. As in the case of the royal official's son, Jesus' word of healing begins the process of the boy's recovery at the very moment Jesus pronounced him well (John 4:52-53). Despite the geographical distance, Jesus' prayers and pronouncement create a tipping point from death to life. Prayer changes us, the pray-ers, as well. Our prayers open our hearts to God's action in our lives, subtly awakening healthy energies of body, mind, and spirit. We are blessed when we bless others. As the story of the Syrophoenecian woman indicates, prayer also opens us to God's presence in strangers, enemies, and intimate friends and relationships. Prayer – or distant healing – reminds us that we live in a world of interdependence in which most of our boundaries are the result of self-interest, greed, ancient antagonisms, and alienation. Prayer heals our hearts and reminds us that we are one in the spirit whether we sitting side by side or across the planet.

HEALING MARKS

In this section, we explore two questions related to our quality of life and spiritual practices: 1) What are you saying? and 2) For whom are you praying? Our words, whether prayerful, blessings, or curses can change the world and the lives of those around us.

Philippians 4 counsels us to think about these things – the good, true, noble, and positive. What we think about ourselves and others – our inner dialogues or self-talk – can limit or liberate. So, too, our words can shape the realities of others. The old adage, "sticks and stones can break my bones, but words will never hurt me" is simply wrong. Negative language about gender, sexuality, race, ethnicity, intelligence, weight, or appearance can destroy self-confidence and lead to hopelessness and violence. Hate speech not only deadens the spirit of those who are attacked but minimizes God's ability to be present in the lives of those whose language alienates and demeans.

In this time of spiritual examination, consider the words you use to describe "others" – people who differ in race, ethnicity, gender, sexuality, age, and so on. Do these words edify or harm, support or malign? In your household, do you speak words of sensitivity, support, love, and encouragement? How do you respond when you are frustrated or angry? Do you strike out with words that demean or do you take a breath, compose yourself, and speak carefully and rationally when you are upset?

None of us are perfect. We all fall short in terms of language, but mindful and self-aware speech enables us to be helpful when we are tempted to be most hurtful. Our language should contribute to healing rather than pain in the lives of others. After this time of prayerful reflection, ask God for a healing of your speech, in the spirit of the Psalm: "Let the words of my mouth and the meditations of my heart be acceptable in your sight, O God, my strength and my redeemer."

For whom are you praying? Do you pray for others at all? While there is no one style of intercessory prayer – some people use words, others images, still others visualize positive outcomes or see Jesus beside the one for whom they pray. Take time in this exercise to find a place of calm and spiritual openness. Ask God to speak within your life, giving you guidance for whom you should pray. As you rest in God's presence, let images of people flow into your mind. As an image arises, take time to pray for God's blessing on that person.

You may choose to make a prayer list, either using words or pictures. You may also choose to pray generally as well as intimately for your Facebook friends or for each person you with whom you correspond online.

CHAPTER SEVEN

HEALING TAKES TIME

They came to Bethsaida. Some people brought a blind man to him and begged him to touch him. [23] He took the blind man by the hand and led him out of the village; and when he had put saliva on his eyes and laid his hands on him, he asked him, "Can you see anything?" And the man looked up and said, [24] "I can see people, but they look like trees, walking." [25] Then Jesus laid his hands on his eyes again; and he looked intently and his sight was restored, and he saw everything clearly. [26] Then he sent him away to his home, saying, "Do not even go into the village." – Mark 8:22-26

When Healing Doesn't Come. Janet came to my seminary study with a host of questions. She had been a student in my course on the healings of Jesus and had been a pivotal person in initiating a healing service in her congregation. She had experienced God's healing touch that delivered her from debilitating migraine head-aches, but recently had been struggling with the contrast between her experience of healing and her congregation's low key healing service and the flamboyant approach of the television healers, where a mere touch often leads to people throwing away their glasses, falling on the floor "slain in the spirit," and getting up from their wheelchairs. Janice confessed, "What's wrong with our church? People feel greater peace after the service, but no one experiences anything dramatic. When folks watch the television healers, every-one seems to be cured, and no one ever dies. Do they have more faith? Do they have more healing power? Or, is it some kind of group hypnosis or placebo effect? Why doesn't someone jump out of their wheelchair at our church?" Needless to say, we had plenty to talk about!

Recently, I was asked to preach on the subject of healing at a large Episcopal church. They, too, were beginning a healing ministry and wanted me to lead a retreat and pave the way for their programmatic initiatives. But I was reminded about the holiness and responsibility of the preacher's task when I looked out from my pulpit and saw six people in wheelchairs sitting in the handicapped section, right in front of the pulpit. I knew that easy answers and platitudes, invoking the power of prayer and healing faith to unambiguously and immediately invoke God's healing would be spiritually harmful and insensitive to my listeners. Life simply doesn't work that way, nor do our healing prayers. I suspected that these people had prayed, gone to physicians, and possibly even healing services, but were still confined to their wheelchairs and, in the case of those in the congregation with ALS, could only look forward to further physical impairment and eventual death apart from a dramatic cure.

I respect the work of many Christian faith healers and non-Christian alternative healers. Many of these people have been touched by God in unique ways or have discovered healing methodologies that transform peoples' lives and relieve suffering. Some simply stayed out of the way and let God's healing energy flow through them, sharing God's gifts without fanfare or notoriety. I am sure that although we are all called to be God's healing partners, some persons have unique or superlative gifts of healing touch and presence. Still, I think the dramatic programs and extravagant claims of televangelists often do a disservice to everyday people involved in their congregation's healing services or seeking healing for themselves or their loved ones. In spotlighting successes, they may cause spiritual harm to those who don't get well or whose healing process plateaus prior to full recovery. They assume they are failures or that God doesn't care, because nothing appears to change in their health conditions or personal finances.

Like politics, healing has become big business. The simplicity of small town churches and traveling tent meetings has given way to high tech fundraising, professional hair stylists, Hollywood-style sets, and dramatic presentations. In the course of our conversation about television healers, Janet noted, "The faith healers never fail on television. Everyone's cured and lives happily ever after. Right then and there, everything changes. That can't be real, at least not all of the time. Real life is a mixture of success and failure. These healers appear to have a better success rate than Jesus; after all, he had trouble in Nazareth and then there was that blind man in Bethsaida. How come it took Jesus two tries to get it right?" She added, "I thank God each day for the healing of my migraines but that took months of prayer, meditation, and laying on of hands, and I still needed the help of medication."

She had a point. While the television healers always say that "it's God, not me," they never trot out the ambiguous cases, the temporary healings, and those who leave with the same problems that they brought them to begin with. Many of them have achieved "rock star status" and the lifestyles that accompany success and celebrity. Moreover, though they preach that everything points to God, the televangelist is regularly touted as a special conduit of blessing, far superior to your local pastor or healing team.

Running an international media ministry requires significant financial support. In big business, after all, you don't highlight your failures. If you want the money to roll in – and it costs a lot in salaries, perquisites, advertising, and technology to maintain a first class television ministry – you have to advertise a 100% success rate, or at least minimize your failures. You have to hype the program to elicit the placebo effect that at the very least gives people short term palliation. As Janet complained, "When was the last time one of these healers preached about their failures or the people who don't get well?"

While using the internet, social networking, and television is appropriate in our technological and global village, the simplicity of Jesus' healing touch and gentle conversation seems to have been obscured by professional marketers, credit card offering plates, electronic communication, and constant appeals for financial support. The story of Jesus' encounter with the sight-impaired man reminds us that the healing process can be as simple as a kind word, a gentle touch, and a persistent prayer.

Gentle, Gradual Healing. In Mark's story of a man healed of blindness, Jesus takes a very different approach from the public displays of healing characteristic of today's tele-healers. The story begins and ends in solitude. Jesus takes the man away from the village and its gossips, prying eyes, and preconceptions of this sight-impaired man. Jesus doesn't want this healing encounter to be a spectacle, nor, given the impact disbelief has on the citizens of Nazareth on Jesus' healing power, does he want the locals' disbelief to get in the way of the sight-impaired man's personal and physical transformation.

While we don't fully know the nature of this healing encounter, Jesus' healing modality involves using natural healing modalities in partnership with prayer. Believed by Jesus' contemporaries to have curative powers, spittle was akin to today's antibiotic ointments or other medicinal poultices. Yet, the natural and the divine are not in conflict with one another. The One who creates pharmaceuticals can use medication in tandem with meditation, prayer, and laying on of hands. We can't separate God's aim at healing into separate spheres: the medicinal and spiritual, or technological and personal. The whole earth is spiritual, permeated as it is by God's wisdom and aim at wholeness and beauty. If God is truly omnipresent, then latent within every moment is the possibility of healing and transformation. Every healing method, including secular Western medicine and spirit-oriented Eastern medicine can be seen as sacramental.

What happens next is surprising to many readers, though a source of consolation to persons who deal with chronic illness and deferred answers to prayer. The man is not cured: he can see but his sight is blurred, "I can see people, but they look like trees, walking." I believe that Mark includes this story as an image of hope: God heals in ordinary as well as dramatic ways. No doubt, many of the first Christians, like people today, felt let down at having to live with long-term chronic illness. They needed to know that

God had not abandoned them despite the apparent lack of a cure or the reality of modest improvements. They needed to see healing as a gradual process, similar in kind to the smallest mustard seed growing into a great plant or the seed thrown on the ground that grows one hundredfold, while other seeds are choked by weeds or scorched by sun. Healing happens, but there is no predictable pathway to human wholeness. It takes faith to wait!

Despite the apparent failure, Jesus does not give up, nor does he blame the sight impaired man for his partial healing. Jesus doesn't look for a reason in the man's lack of faith, God's will, or divine punishment. He simply continues with the healing process, once more touching the man's eyes prayerfully and lovingly. Jesus' approach is a far cry from Ed's experience. When he had a recurrence of colon cancer, ironically his Christian and new age friends had similar explanations. His Christian friend accused him of not having enough faith. "If only you trusted God, repented of your sins, and had more faith, you'd be fine. You've simply got to believe God." Another friend, a follower of new age guru Louise Hay, was certain that the recurrence of cancer was a "lesson to be learned." She asked Ed, "What is it you need to learn from your cancer? What are you holding onto that brought the cancer back? My teacher says that cancer is related to emotional blocks and negative thinking. Is there something you can't 'stomach' that's caused the colon cancer? Are you 'blocked' somewhere?" Ed found both of these explanations hurtful and appalling.

When we met for coffee, he angrily announced, "I thought these people were my friends, but with friends like these, who needs enemies?" Over several months, Ed and I met for coffee and conversation. I prayed with him and taught him how to meditate. I also taught him the use of spiritual affirmations and visualization techniques to accompany his chemotherapy treatments. Gradually, Ed's condition improved. Today, he is married, cancer free and the parent of two young children. He is grateful for his medical care, but he affirms that "without prayer and meditation, I might not have made it. Learning that cancer was value neutral and that God was on my side and I was not to blame for my illness gave me the courage to continue despite the side effects of the treatment and my fears of dying."

Jesus' healing of the sight-impaired man provides a positive model for our own healing ministries. Jesus persists in healing prayer. He is patient with the process of recovery. Perhaps, Jesus recognizes – as many people do following surgery – that this man needs to grow into his healing. After surgery, you don't immediately get up and run. You begin with small steps on the road to good health. This man needs to begin to see himself as a sighted person once more. He needs a retreat from the curious crowd and its judgments to insure that his vision has time to go from opaque to clear in terms of eyesight and self-awareness. He may need to figure out what he is to do for a living, now that he no longer depends on his family and the kindness of strangers. After all, healing may create new "problems." As we overcome old limitations, we need to take on new responsibilities and a new identity, and that also takes time and effort.

In the spirit of the woman who persistently took her case to the "unjust judge" of Jesus' parable, patience with prayer and persistence in our quest for wholeness can be the tipping point between health and illness, and life and death (Luke 18:1-8). I must admit that there are times that I become bored with my petitions and intercessions. Month after month I pray for the same people and certain issues in my own life, and yet they remain unresolved. But, then, I step back and recognize that even if my condition doesn't immediately change, my prayers transform my attitude. They help me live with what is beyond my control and take responsibility for what is within my power. Moreover, as I go through my daily prayer list – and some dear friends, living with cancer and other health problems, have been the object of my prayers for a number of years – I affirm that my prayers create a field of force that enhances their well-being, longevity, and God's ability to bring new energies into their situations. They also signify the love I have for them, a love that is stronger than death. Who knows what would happen if I quit praying? Frankly, I'm not going to take the chance!

As one friend confessed to me, "I'm grateful that you pray for me each day. I know your prayers have made a difference. They've helped me face incurable cancer and, I believe, that they've made a difference in my health." My friend's future is still in doubt in terms of his illness, but our community of prayer has sustained his hope that life is beautiful and God has the final word in his life, and that word is always love! Even though, they haven't cured his cancer, they may have kept it at bay and bolstered his spirits for the long haul.

There are no guarantees that our prayers will secure the miracles we hope for. But I am convinced that the consistency and persistency of our prayers helps those for whom we pray live well and ultimately die well, enabling them to know that whether we live or die we belong forever with God.

We can persist in prayer because God is faithful. God's mercies are new every morning. Yes, every morning, God is faithful, and not just in the dramatic moments of life. In the gentle movements of the immune system, in wounds healing and broken bones knitted together, in the healing of memories and trauma, in the flow of chemotherapy and the focus of radiation, there is a persistent divine movement, slowly but surely revealing the love that gives life to cells and souls, and day after day sustains planets and galaxies. Even if our condition plateaus and improvement stops or the dreaded cancer returns, our prayers connect us with a field of divine healing that gives us the serenity to face what can't be changed and live fully despite a negative prognosis.

HEALING MARKS

Healing involves persistence, and the willingness to come day after day in relationship to God through prayer. As you look at your life and relationships, for whom are you called to pray? What issues in your life invite prayer? In the spirit of Jairus' daughter, consider becoming part of a healing team even if it involves only one other person. For example, I pray for my best friend as she faces serious health issues every morning as I take my sunrise walk. I know that she wakes up about the same time and prays for me and my personal and professional well-being. I pray for my grandson every morning and throughout the day. I have a number of other people on my prayer list.

I encourage you to create your own prayer list and regularly pray for the persons on your list. One of the more poignant moments of my life was discovering as I tidied up his house after my father's debilitating stroke that he had a long list of people for whom he prayed each day. I believe that my father, Everett, still prayed for those people from his wheel chair in the nursing home, although now his prayers came from the unconscious, that place of "sighs too deep for words" where our spirit and God's Spirit meet. Though our prayers may not appear to be immediately answered, I believe they make a difference in the health of persons and the planet. What would the world be like – and what would happen to your loved ones – if you quit praying? Do you remember Frank Capra's Christmas film, *It's a Wonderful Life*? The absence of one life, or perhaps, even one prayer can change the world. Conversely, the presence of just this one prayer can tip the balance between health and illness, hope and hopelessness, and life and death, for us and our loved ones. While it never fully depends on us – and our forgetfulness is compensated by God's grace – no one can quantify the impact of our prayers.

Creating a prayer list is simple. Just write down people's names. Be prepared to add names. Take a moment each day to review the list, prayerfully saying the name or visualizing each person on your list. Conversely, consider reaching out to a prayer partner with whom you will pray for each other. We don't need to be pious about our prayers, but there is a comfort in knowing that somebody is praying for you, consistently, persistently, and patiently in all the routine, ongoing, and critical issues of life.

CHAPTER EIGHT

HEALING BROKEN SPIRITS

They came to the other side of the sea, to the country of the Gerasenes. ²And when he had stepped out of the boat, immediately a man out of the tombs with an unclean spirit met him. ³He lived among the tombs; and no one could restrain him anymore, even with a chain; ⁴for he had often been restrained with shackles and chains, but the chains he wrenched apart, and the shackles he broke in pieces; and no one had the strength to subdue him. ⁵Night and day among the tombs and on the mountains he was always howling and bruising himself with stones. ⁶When he saw Jesus from a distance, he ran and bowed down before him; ⁷and he shouted at the top of his voice, "What have you to do with me, Jesus, Son of the Most High God? I adjure you by God, do not torment me." ⁸For he had said to him, "Come out of the man, you unclean spirit!" ⁹Then Jesus asked him, "What is your name?" He replied, "My name is Legion; for we are many." ¹⁰He begged him earnestly not to send them out of the country. ¹¹Now there on the hillside a great herd of swine was feeding; ¹²and the unclean spirits begged him, "Send us into the swine; let us enter them." ¹³So he gave them permission. And the unclean spirits came out and entered the swine; and the herd, numbering about two thousand, rushed down the steep bank into the sea, and were drowned in the sea.

¹⁴The swineherds ran off and told it in the city and in the country. Then people came to see what it was that had happened. ¹⁵They came to Jesus and saw the demoniac sitting there, clothed and in his right mind, the very man who had had the legion; and they were afraid. ¹⁶Those who had seen what had happened to the demoniac and to the swine reported it. ¹⁷Then they began to beg Jesus to leave their neighborhood. ¹⁸As he was getting into the boat, the man who had been possessed by demons begged him that he might be with him. ¹⁹But Jesus refused, and said to him, "Go

*home to your friends, and tell them how much the Lord has done
for you, and what mercy he has shown you." [20]And he went away
and began to proclaim in the Decapolis how much Jesus had done
for him; and everyone was amazed. – Mark 5:1-20*

Losing Control and Experiencing Grace. For most of my
life, I have enjoyed mental and emotional equanimity. I typically
respond to stress by meditating, walking, praying, and looking
for a larger perspective within which to place the challenges and
failures of life. But, recently, I had an unexpected unsettling and
stressful experience. For no apparent physiological reason, I had
trouble getting a complete breath. For two days, I couldn't catch
my breath. I became anxious when none of my typical responses to
stress made any difference. Never a victim of insomnia in the past,
I could only muster a few hours sleep for two nights running, and
this was on the eve of an important job interview. In retrospect, I
realized that I had experienced a mild anxiety attack.

Experiencing an anxiety attack was a learning experience, because for the first time in my life, I felt emotionally out of control
and unable to find a solution to my problem by my own efforts.
The following Monday, I made an emergency appointment with
my physician and, after talking with her for half an hour, realized
that between leaving my position at the seminary, job hunting,
and responding to my brother's unexpected death, I was under
more stress than I realized. No doubt, the prospect of a job interview tipped my unconscious from equanimity to uncertainty,
which was reflected in my sense of physical well-being. Just to be
on the safe side, I requested a prescription for mild anti-anxiety
medication and also a sleeping medication. While I haven't used
the sleeping medication, it has served as a security blanket in case
I had a repetition of insomnia. I'm uncertain about the benefits of
an anti-anxiety medication, but I am a firm believer in prayer and
Prozac and meditation and medication as instruments of God's
healing power. I prayerfully take my medication right after I meditate each morning.

Needless to say, this has been a spiritual lesson, which has increased my understanding of my brother and mother, both of whom dealt with mental health issues for four decades. I also feel a kinship and sense of empathy with others who regularly experience anxiety attacks or disorders which temporarily immobilize them or make everyday tasks challenging. I discovered God's grace and a greater sensitivity for others in the midst of my feelings of weakness and loss of control.

Unclean Spirits? Have you noticed that in spite of the modern world's identification of angels and demons with superstition and its medicalization of mental health issues, there has been a proliferation of movies about spirit-possession, demonic entitities, and vampires, not to mention movies and television programs describing angelic companions, in the past few decades? Deep down, I suspect this is a result of our realization that we are not at the pinnacle of the evolutionary ladder. We imagine the possibility of superior beings, both positive and negative, who influence our lives and world history. Further, despite the Enlightenment and modern world's emphasis on rationality and conscious control, we have a dim awareness of a multi-layered universe, reflected in the multi-layered nature of human experience. Moreover, interest in the demonic testifies to the often-suppressed reality that we are never fully in control of our emotional or mental health. Rationality and consciousness are, as both Jung and Freud pointed out, the tip of the iceberg beneath which is a world of unconscious drives, repressed memories, non-rational experiences, dreams and nightmares, and angelic and demonic influences. Whether or not we believe in such spiritual entities, we are always only a few steps from entering "the twilight zone."

Modern psychology has unearthed the impact of addiction and trauma on our well-being. Physical, emotional, and spiritual or ritual abuse, can lead to post-traumatic stress and in certain extreme cases dissociative disorders, popularly referred to as multiple personality disorders. In such cases, the centered self is "split" into a variety of personalities that operate independently and often at cross purposes with one another. Further, while spiritual realities fall outside of the province of mainstream medicine and psychology, there are rare instances in which people believe that they are possessed by forces outside themselves whose intent is malevolent and destructive. These forces, or alters, may have different names, likes and dislikes, vocal tones, and allergies than each other and the "presiding personality." The Roman Catholic Church has a special ordination among priests who are called to serve as exorcists, that is, persons trained to identify, confront, and cast out demons following the model of Jesus of Nazareth.

While these experiences and the realities toward which they point remain mysterious, and can be described in both spiritual and medical terms, we can never underestimate their impact on the human psyche nor can we overestimate our ability to be in full control of unconscious energies, images, and influences moving through our lives. Sophisticated twenty-first century persons need only recall how one of the most cultured countries in the world, Germany, was possessed by "demonic" forces and controlled by the fancies of a charismatic and mentally unstable leader or how quickly mob violence can erupt in an otherwise quiet community. What happened during the diabolical "Third Reich" has also reappeared in the irrational group behaviors of soldiers at My Lai during the Vietnam War, the Cambodian genocide during the Pol Pot regime, and the tribal massacres in Africa. Otherwise normal people, finding themselves grasped by the "group mind," appear to be possessed by "powers and principalities" that drive them to uncharacteristic acts of violence.

In the first century, many diseases such as epilepsy were seen as forms of spirit possession. In fact, epilepsy was known as the "sacred disease" because it took people out of themselves in an apparently mystical state. The spirit possessed boy described in Mark 9:14-29 appears to have all the symptoms of what today we would describe as epilepsy. If this is the case, and the spirit that "possessed" him was the modern disease of epilepsy, this does not diminish the impact of Jesus' healing prayer. Different eras have different names for disease. Persons once described as "shell shocked" are now diagnosed in terms of "post-traumatic stress." The "lazy" or "misbehaving and unfocussed" child or adult of a generation ago may be diagnosed with depression or some form of attention deficit hyperactivity disorder. Homosexuality was once seen as a mental illness; today, it is understood in non-clinical, non-ethical, and non-pejorative ways by persons educated in health care and the human condition. In the spirit of the medical modalities of *Star Trek*, no doubt, future generations will see our diagnoses, words for illness, and treatment plans as primitive compared to their own.

Too Many Spirits! The story of the demon-possessed man, recorded in Mark 5:1-20, follows Mark's account of the storm at sea (Mark 4:36-41). In many ways they are companion stories, describing our panic at being out of control, whether through the impact of natural forces or inner psychological states. This is especially true in light of Carl Jung's identification of dreams involving the sea pointing to the power of the unconscious mind. Yet, whether we find ourselves in violent tsunamis of the spirit or the quiet storms of panic, Christ is in the boat, reminding us with the British mystic Julian of Norwich that "all will be well and all manner of thing will be well."

The story of the Gerasene demoniac joins the spiritual, demonic, emotional, ethnic, relational, and political elements of life. Once again, Jesus is at the end of his settled world; many scholars identify the Gerasa as one of the ten Gentile cities of the Decapolis. Jesus is traveling through the chaotic and spiritually and politically dangerous world of the Gentile oppressors. Further, many Bible scholars note that when Mark's readers heard the word "legion," their first association would be Roman occupying troops, numbering typically between two and six thousand. Despite the oppressor's violent rule and near omnipotent power over them, Jesus' Jewish contemporaries identified Romans as unclean, evil, and demonic. In addition, political upheaval and oppression can lead to greater stress and mental instability in troubled communities. Following the terrorist attacks of September 11, 2001, many residents of Manhattan, Northern New Jersey, and Washington D.C. experienced increased stress that required medication.

Could it be that this man's mental instability was exacerbated by the powerlessness he felt in relationship to the heartless, arbitrary and violent Roman occupation troops? Or, could he have been a Gentile, whose physiological and mental health issues had rendered him a virtual non-person among his fellow Gentiles? As many of us know, mental health disorders can alienate, isolate, impoverish, and lead to homelessness or institutionalization.

As Mark's story goes, Jesus is met by a man possessed by thousands of demons. In his time, diagnosis of demon possession was akin to modern medicine's germ theory, an external force that took over a person's psyche, causing disorders of mind, body, and spirit. This particular demonic force, apparently guided by a central demon, had so dominated the man that he had lost his centralized, presiding personality. His mental illness was reflected in superhuman strength, uncontrollable movements, and irrational shrieks. He is no longer considered fully human; he lives in the graveyard, for all intents and purposes, dead to the larger community and those who once loved him. Like many street persons today, whether military veterans, substance abusers, or refugees from institutionalization, he has lost his name, his power, and his position. He is a nuisance and nobody, and a threat to himself and others.

Much to the surprise of the crowd that has gathered to view his encounter with the healer, the demon-possessed man identifies Jesus as uniquely related to God, the Son of the Most High, whose aim is to restore their "host" to emotional and social well-being. While Mark does not describe in detail Jesus' technique of exorcism, the demons recognize that they soon will be homeless and make an audacious request. "Send us into the swine, let us enter them." They experience Jesus' quest for healing as torment, just as recovery from certain types of surgery and chemotherapy can be perceived as worse than the ailment until we discover how necessary these medical procedures are to our recovery. Much to the demons' surprise, Jesus agrees to their request. Sickness must go somewhere, in this case into the "unclean" pigs. Was Jesus casting the demons into the swine an act of liberation for both the man and the demons? Were the unclean spirits somehow cleansed or healed in the process?

The encounter of Jesus and the demons raises some further interesting questions: If God is omnipresent, is there a movement toward health subtly present even within mental health disorders? Does the God who seeks abundant life for all creation work subtly through our neuroses and disorders of body, mind, and spirit luring them, perhaps even against their will, toward wholeness? Can demonic spirits, if such exists, also hear the gospel and experience redemption?

The issue in this story is not the dangers of complexity of experience. Creativity and imagination require complexity and dissonance with social and religious norms and limits. Roberto Assagioli, a student of Jung, developed a psychological theory called "psychosynthesis" in which he explored the many sub-personalities that comprise the life of every healthy or neurotic person.[1] Elizabeth O'Connor adapted psychosynthesis to the Christian quest for integrity of spirit in her book, *Our Many Selves.*[2] We are all legion, to some extent, and our complexity is the source of imagination, creativity, and empathy as well as neuroses. Still, as the Danish philosopher Soren Kierkegaard asserted, "purity of heart is to will one thing," that is, to find a spiritual center around which to integrate the complexity of our inner life and daily experiences. When Jesus banished the demonic forces that had dominated this man's life, the man's spiritual, personal, and emotional center was restored. Once completely disoriented, he now has a new orientation, grounded in the healing acts of Jesus. He was, as Mark says, "clothed and in his right mind." He wants to follow Jesus, but Jesus challenges him to take his healing home as a testimony to God's touch. Those

---

1 Roberto Assaglioli, *Psychosynthesis* (Amherst, MA: The Synthesis Center, 2000).

2 Elizabeth O'Connor, *Our Many Selves* (New York: Harper Collins, 1971).

who once knew him as mentally disordered and possessed by forces outside himself would be challenged by his spiritual transformation to explore their own well-being and relationship with God. Healing is about coming home to your deepest self and relationship with God and your neighbor. His healing is also a witness to the loving power of God to transform our lives when we most vulnerable and at risk. One further thought: Could this man have been Jesus' first Gentile disciple, sharing the good news at the grassroots level rather than on foot throughout the region?

The Problem with Healing. We might have expected exuberant celebration from the crowd. Yet, as Mark notes, the locals "began to beg Jesus to leave the neighborhood." While we can't fully discern their intent, many of the locals recognized that a proliferation of healing would transform people and communities, and change their way of life and possibly their economic situation. It might even threaten the political and economic status quo. The healing of persons can be costly in terms of time, talent, and treasure. In order for justice to be done, sacrifices must be made. To achieve an overall improvement in community health, we need to adjust economic and governmental spending and priorities, and often we resist what is necessary for realizing Martin Luther King's dream of a "beloved community" of mutual affirmation, justice, well-being, and equality.

The locals' desire for Jesus to leave betrays their worry that if Jesus cures too many people, the social order will be upset and the Romans may intervene, threatening their incomes and lifestyle. They would rather live with an acceptable number of sick people, both mentally and physical ill, than upset the social order or make the sacrifices necessary for all people to be treated with care and consideration.

Today, we have to ask ourselves if we have any resistance to personal and social manifestations of God's healing touch in our midst. While I recognize the importance of issues of freedom as related to diet and personal choice, the wider social order sends messages to people that encourage obesity, substance abuse, consumerism, and poor health. Changing these messages will improve the overall well-being of millions of our fellow citizens. Further, the United States seems complacent in terms of accessible health care and quality education for all its citizens. Some politicians even resist governmental regulations related to healthier school lunches. These issues beg questions such as: How much are we willing to sacrifice economically for the well-being of our fellow citizens, especially children? How do we balance personal and corporate freedom with the need for prevention especially when better health demands greater regulation of advertising and product placement? What is the role of the church in preventing illness – for example, obesity, diabetes, and high blood pressure – in our communities? Are we being hypocritical as Christian leaders, when we emphasize liturgical healing services and pray for the healing of people whose illnesses could have been prevented by better diet, accessible health care, and quality education and job training? How are we responding to persons suffering from mental illness and substance abuse in our midst, whether in our community or congregation?

Mountaintop Experiences and Desperate Parents. Mark boldly proclaims the interplay of mysticism and mission. Faith without works and contemplation without action is incomplete and irrelevant to the pain of the world. In the account of the transfiguration of Jesus, Jesus, Peter, James, and John go to the mountaintop, where Jesus is transfigured. He is dazzling as he reflects and radiates the energy of the universe and the power from which all healing comes. Jesus enters into dialogue with Moses and Elijah, the supreme figures of Jewish spirituality and receives a spoken blessing from the living God. Alas, ecstatic mystical experiences don't last forever. Jesus and his followers must go down the mountain toward confrontation in Jerusalem. They are met by a distraught and desperate father, whose son has experienced seizures, not unlike grand mal epilepsy, from childhood. He is a threat to himself during his seizures, falling down, foaming, convulsing, and grinding his teeth.

After years of dealing with his son's disease, the father has almost given up hope; in fact, Jesus may be his last hope. He pleads for a healing for his beloved child, trusting God in spite of all his doubts: "I believe; help my unbelief."

Our faith does not need to be perfect or unambiguous to make a difference. Theologian Paul Tillich asserts that authentic faith always includes an element of doubt.[1] "All things can be done for the one who believes," so proclaims Jesus (Mark 9:23). A mustard seed's faith can move a mountain, and the greatest faith often flourishes when we accept our whole self in all our complexity, ambivalence, and fear. Like this boy's father, we don't have to deny our struggles to receive God's grace. God's healing touch, restoring spirits as well as bodies, comes in times of conflict and uncertainty as well as consolation and peace. As the hymn goes:

> Through many dangers, toils and snares
> I have already come;
> 'Tis Grace that brought me safe thus far
> and Grace will lead me home.[2]

Going home means returning to our loved ones, whether a man in midlife or a young child with his whole life ahead of him. Jesus' healing always provides a pathway home, whether home is the place of our origin or the hope of the future.

HEALING MARKS

Jesus' ministry to spirit-possessed persons challenges us to become active in responding to issues of mental illness and substance abuse in our communities.[3] This involves education, advocacy, and action. It also involves confronting the stigma of mental illness, whether among fellow congregants or in the wider community.

---

1 Paul Tillich, *The Dynamics of Faith* (New York: Harper, 1958).
2 John Newton, "Amazing Grace." (1779)
3 Gerald May, *Addiction and Grace* (San Francisco: Harper One, 2007).

Given the reality of post-traumatic stress among veterans of the wars in Iran and Afghanistan, this also involves a commitment to respond individually, congregationally, and politically in ways that support the well-being of our military, including Vietnam war veterans. Looking at your own congregation: Does your congregation have a mission toward persons with mental health issues? In what way is your congregation involved in mental health issues in the larger community?

As a spiritual practice, make it a habit to visualize and identify persons with obvious mental health issues as beloved children of God. See the angels hidden within the boulders of mental illness. Experience God's light shining from within them, regardless of their symptoms. As Mother Teresa counsels, look for Christ hidden in all of his distressing disguises. Bring forth God's image in such persons by your prayers, respect, and affirmative care.

CHAPTER NINE

HEALING AND BLESSING

People were bringing little children to him in order that he might touch them; and the disciples spoke sternly to them. [14]*But when Jesus saw this, he was indignant and said to them, "Let the little children come to me; do not stop them; for it is to such as these that the kingdom of God belongs.* [15]*Truly I tell you, whoever does not receive the kingdom of God as a little child will never enter it."* [16]*And he took them up in his arms, laid his hands on them, and blessed them.* – Mark 10:13-16

Everyone needs a blessing! Jon knocked on my study door, shaking and in tears. Once again, he had felt judged by his father, for whom nothing he did ever seemed good enough. Despite the fact that Jon was successful in business, he never received any affirmation from his father. As a child, he excelled in school and sports, but his father always noticed the dropped pass, the strikeout, or the A-, rather than a touchdown, home run, or graduation *cum laude*. In the course of thirty years, Jon had seldom heard a word of praise, or an "I love you" from his father. He recognized that his father believed that words of praise and love spoiled a child and made a man soft and sentimental rather than tough and aggressive. Still, Jon needed a blessing. "I want to know that my father loves me and, lacking that, was at least minimally proud of what I've done with my life. I feel unworthy of his love, and keep trying to get it." He had set the bar for receiving his father's blessing exceedingly low – just a slight acknowledgment would have thrilled him – and still had not receive the affirmation for which he hungered.

Jon and I had a number of long talks at the local coffee house over the few months. I kept reminding him that regardless of what his father said, God's words to Jesus at his baptism applied to him as well, "You are my son, the Beloved, with you I am well pleased" (Mark 1:11). Even if his father never showed Jon his love, there was another parent, who loved him without reservation. He didn't need to earn God's love; it was always there for the receiving with no minimal requirements, bars to jump over, or tests to pass. But, Jon also needed to experience a "God with skin," so each time we met, we parted with the traditional blessing from Numbers 6:24-26:

> *The Lord bless you and keep you;* ²⁵*the Lord make his face to shine upon you, and be gracious to you;* ²⁶*the Lord lift up his countenance upon you, and give you peace.*

I concluded the traditional blessing with a hug and my personal blessing. "You are God's beloved child, you are loved, and you are good." Jon never received the blessing he sought from his father, but he experienced the deeper blessing of companionship with God and the healing power of an accepting relationship from another male authority figure. Today, while he still deals with occasional issues of self-worth, Jon is able to give and receive love, and recognize the value of his work and his relationships apart from anyone else's approval.

The Healing Power of Blessing. There is a virtue in vagueness, especially when it comes to life's most important issues. There is no one way to bless, nor is there a precise definition of blessing. In the biblical tradition, whether it involves blessing the meek or mourning (Matthew 5:1-12) or the blessings received by Jacob (Genesis 28:10-17; 32:21-32) and Abraham and Sarah (Genesis 12:1-4), blessing involves a sense of God's favor and care. God is not indifferent to our lives, but wants all of us to flourish and prosper. The scriptures speak of blessings in terms of prosperity and good fortune, but more than that a sense of inner peace, joy, and wholeness for oneself and one's loved ones.

For the past year, I have made a commitment to bless the world. As I walk through my neighborhood each morning, I bless the residents as I go by their homes. I also pray for friends far and near. I take a moment to say a word of kindness to the grocery store or pharmacy clerk, and often pronounce an internal blessing upon them. I give an inner – and sometimes spoken – blessing to every baby I encounter. In a world in which cursing – and wishing ill – comes so easily, a word of blessing is countercultural. Accordingly, I have made it a point to bless every situation, whether it is joyful or challenging. When I am tempted to diminish another, I make it a point to bless them, even if I disagree with them politically, ethically, or theologically. Blessing connects, while cursing alienates, first in our hearts and then in our words and actions. The widespread reality of the culture wars and their impact on congregational unity, worship, politics, and race relations – is a testimony to the impact of cursing on church, family, and society.

In the spirit of the ancient blessing, I often say a silent prayer in greeting or saying goodbye: "May the Lord bless you and keep you. May the Lord make his face to shine upon you and be gracious unto you. May the Lord lift up his countenance upon you and give you peace." While you may choose to substitute "God" or "Christ" to make the blessing more inclusive, the point is your desire to mediate God's abundance to another person.

To be blessed is to experience abundant life, joy, and well-being regardless of life's circumstances. It is to experience the world as a place of beauty, wonder, and holiness. Being blessed involves a sense of connection with the life-giving energy of the Universe and the Spirit that gives life to all things regardless of your life situation. To bless is to be a conscious agent and companion in God's quest to heal the world. I want to be blessed, but more importantly I want to bless – bless people, animals, situations, and the world. I want to make a difference in healing relationships and upbuilding my community, and blessing is the key to transforming our world.

Blessings make a difference in body, mind, and spirit. They change our way of looking at the world. These days, as I go from task to task in the course of a busy day, I often invoke the Navajo prayer, "With blessings all around me, I walk." This enables me to give as well as receive blessings throughout the day.

Blessing changes your perception of everyday encounters. It enlivens your steps and enhances your energy; it also brings beauty and abundance, crucial factors in the healing process, to those around us. When we feel blessed, we can face life's challenges knowing that we are not alone and that we have the relational and personal resources to respond to every need. "With blessings all around us, we walk."

Blessing the Children. In Kathryn Stockett's book - and the film version - *The Help,* Aibileen, who serves as the family house-keeper, reminds Mae Mobley, a neglected preschooler of her value with the words, "You is kind. You is smart. You is important." Like Jesus, this humble housekeeper is pronouncing the radical blessing of prophetic hospitality. In contrast, to her privileged and educated employers, she tells a neglected child that she is beloved and that regardless of her parents' relationship with her, she matters – to her caregiver Aibileen and ultimately to God whose love envelopes and guides her.

When Jesus blessed the children, he was not just being sweet, he was being prophetic. In the first century, many parents, such as Jairus and his wife, loved their children. But, given the harsh realities life and childbirth, children were often considered of little account and social value. They – like their mothers – were told to be seen but not heard. The *pater familias,* or male head of the household, had absolute control of the child's life. In most cases, the relationship was "my way or the highway" even until adulthood. Children had no rights, and certainly were placed at the edges of every social situation as virtual non-persons.

True to the social norms regarding children, Jesus' disciples and the crowd feel justified in telling the children to leave Jesus alone without a second thought. The feelings of children were sel-dom considered. They gained their full value only when they came of age and could work, support the family, and – in the case of female children – give birth, especially to male children. No doubt the crowd was scandalized when Jesus took the children on his lap and blessed them, placing them in front of adults, people that truly mattered!

While we don't know the details the story, I suspect Jesus may have told the children a story – perhaps about a lost sheep or a growing plant – reminding them that God loved them – and then touched them, transferring his power and energy to them. I believe that many of these children remembered this encounter for the rest of their lives. Despite the Roman occupation of Israel, they still knew themselves to be God's beloved children.

When I was a child growing up in the California's Salinas Valley, one of our favorite Sunday School songs was:

Jesus loves the little children, all the children of the world.
Red or yellow, black or white, they are precious in his sight.
Jesus loves the little children of the world.[1]

I believed that this song applied to me and it was fortified by the other hymn of my childhood, "Jesus loves me, this I know, for the Bible tells me so."

When Jesus blessed the children, he invited us to see healing as social as well as personal. As a parent and grandparent, I am distressed by studies that indicate that the primary indicator of a child's health is her or his parents' level of education. I am astonished that in the richest country of the world, millions of children live in poverty. They are not to blame for their parents' inability to secure gainful or adequate employment, personal lifestyle, spending habits, or heritage of poverty. Nor are children like my son or grandson morally or spiritually superior because they were born to more affluent parents committed to higher education.

In God's beloved community, children really matter and that means every child, regardless of ethnicity, economics, nation of origin or family of origin. Those of us who seek to be God's healing partners must engage in prevention as well as prayer. We need

1 Clare Herbert Woolston, "Jesus Loves the Little Children."

to pray with our hands as well as our hearts, seeking just public policies that insure better health, provide safe environments, and support hopefulness among children. As God's healing partners, we must eliminate as many factors as possible that will lead to physical illness, economic uncertainty, emotional insecurity, and low self-esteem in children and the adults they will become. We can't solve all the problems we face, and that includes our own. But, we can live by Jewish wisdom, reflected in the story of the lost sheep: when you save one soul, you save the world.

We All Need a Blessing. It is said that "it's never too late to have a happy childhood!" Deep down, we are all children. While we imagine ourselves as self-made and invulnerable, an unexpected accident or health crises can render us vulnerable and dependent. We all need an environment of love, especially in childhood. Many of us still bear the wounds of childhood neglect, abuse, trauma, and impoverishment. Our "inner child" needs healing and affirmation. This involves the "healing of memories," as Dennis and Matthew Linn aptly describe; it is also the healing of possibilities and limitations, since many of the self-imposed limits in life are the result of childhood wounds. We are imprisoned by internalized scripts of pain, limitation, and low self-esteem that we learned in childhood.[1]

Jesus saw the child as the model for approaching God's realm. Jesus asserted as he blessed the children, "for it is to such as these the kingdom of God belongs" (Mark 10:14). Moreover, Jesus promised that "whoever welcomes one child in my name welcomes me, and whoever welcomes me welcomes not me but the one [God] who sent me" (Mark 9:37). Our hospitality and care for children and the child within us connects us with God's vision for our lives and enables us to live more fully in God's realm of Shalom.

---

1 Matthew and Dennis Linn, *Healing Life's Hurts: The Healing of Memories through the Five Stages of Forgiveness* (New York: Paulist Press, 1977) and *The Healing of Memories* (New York: Paulist Press, 1977); Ruth Carter Stapleton, *The Gift of Inner Healing* (Nashville: Word Books, 1977); Kenneth McAll, *Healing the Family Tree* (London: Sheldon Press, 1999).

While Jesus doesn't fully define the unique relationship of children to God, it is clear that our young children possess an innocence, immediacy, and innate joy that characterize God's intent for human life. We cannot go back to a state of perfection, but we can experience the wonder and beauty of each moment. Along with thanksgiving, appreciation is one of the ways we worship God. Rabbi Abraham Joshua Heschel proclaimed that "radical amazement" is one of the greatest spiritual virtues. Amazement, being caught up in the wonder of the moment, is one of the virtues of childhood that we adults often need to recover.

I have spent a lot of time on my knees lately. I'm not just praying; I'm playing with my toddler grandson. We can spend a morning rolling cars on the floor, talking with stuffed dolls, or noticing the intricacies of a piece of furniture. I've also been spending a lot of time looking upward. My grandson loves planes, stars, and the moon. When we leave the house in the evening, his first impulse is to look upward and point at the moon as he shouts "Moon, moon" in his toddler's inflection. Even when I'm away from my grandson, I see the moon, stars, airplanes, cars, flags, and buses with new eyes. They aren't just passing sights; they are opportunities for learning for child and adult alike.

The child lives in the moment and loves in the moment. He knows what he needs. She jumps into your arms when you open the door or when she hears a loud noise. Without thinking about it, the child knows that he or she depends on the love of others and so, in healthy families, children reach out to be comforted, caressed, touched, and loved. I believe Jesus treasured the wonder and innocence of childhood. His parables could speak to toddlers as well as adults. Imagine a child visualizing the growth of a mustard seed or finding a lost toy. Visualize a child understanding how the lost sheep might have felt and identifying with an anxious parent, searching for her or his child. While children need to learn patience and perspective as they grow up, their sense of beauty, wonder, and imagination is a gift of gratitude to God and a model for adults to reclaim.

Sadly, as we grow older, our sense of imagination is stifled. We become realists, living by facts and the bottom line. We become imprisoned by data and self-imposed limitations. We try to impose these limits of imagination and wonder on children so they can fit into the realism of our society. We think we can go it alone, without the help of others. But, God wants us to recognize another – deeper – realism. This is the realism that sees a multitude fed from a few loaves and fish; a great school of fish hidden despite a night of unsuccessful fishing; a lover in a woman caught in a compromising situation; a hero within a disciple's cowardice; beauty in outcast lepers; and a long life ahead for a comatose girl. Freed from narrow realism, we can venture forth into God's horizon of hope and possibility.

Most of us have lost much of the wonder and imagination – the limitless vision – of childhood. Buried in pain and realism, we need a healing of the inner, playful, loving child regardless of our age. Some call this process the healing of memories. Others describe it as the healing of vocation or purpose. In their work with the impact childhood wounds have on adults, the Linn brothers invite us to go back to a painful memory, to remember what it was like and how we felt when someone neglected us, chastised us, frightened us, or humiliated us. We may even remember life-shattering moments of trauma and abuse. Hillary Clinton once invoked the African proverb, "it takes a village to raise a child." It also takes a village of loving friends and, at times, spiritual guides, counselors, and medical professionals to be God's partners in healing the hurt child within. Few of us can break free from childhood limitations on our own. We need communities of care and healing imagination to awaken us to the healthy child within the struggling adult. We need God's loving vision of abundant life.

In the healing of memories, we remember times of pain. But, we also visualize Jesus as our companion, protecting us, feeling our pain, even taking on our pain (feeling the fist of the abuser or the unwanted sexual intrusion for us) and insuring that our emotional and physical needs are addressed. Jesus is the fellow sufferer who understands. This is the meaning of the cross. We can place our childhood pain in the healing hands of Jesus, because he knows what it's like to be abandoned, abused, and humiliated. He was with us in our painful childhood moments and he is with us as we seek healing and wholeness as adults.

We also need the healing of possibilities or a healing of the imagination. As the apostle Paul proclaims, "do not be conformed to this world, but be transformed by the renewing of your minds" (Romans 12:2). We need to let the one who transformed water into wine awaken us to possibilities that lie hidden in every situation. We need to break free from the false limitations we learned in childhood under the guise of realism and discover a deeper realism of healing spirits and bodies, lively life-transforming energies, unleashed imaginations, and empty tombs. Faith is about the gift of a deeper perception in which we discover amid the limitations of our realism that God is working for good in all things.

Jesus' blessing of the children is an invitation for us to be bold in asking for a healing blessing. As Jacob says to his nocturnal visitor, "I will not let you go, unless you bless me" (Genesis 32:26). The story of the healing of sight-impaired Bartimaeus reminds us that blessings invite us to recognize our deepest needs (Mark 10:46-52). When the persistent Bartimaeus is brought to Jesus, Jesus places Bartimaeus in charge of the healing process with the question, "What do you want me to do for you?" The blessing we need may already be here, waiting for us to break free of our limits and state our needs. Yet, being blessed always takes us beyond ourselves: God's blessing challenges us to bless one another and to enter every situation bringing God's benediction rather than divisive cursing. Jesus blessed the little children, and blesses the child within us so that we live with zest, wonder, and open-heartedness despite the wounds of childhood.

HEALING MARKS

In this section, we will explore a variety of blessings, remembering the power of blessing to heal body, mind, spirit, and
relationships. The first is the blessing of intentionality. As you awak-
en in the morning, make a commitment to be a channel of God's
blessing throughout the day. Ask God to give a heart of blessing in
every situation. Bless the people you meet. Most of the time, this
is simply a matter of attitude and prayer. As you encounter people
and situations, pray that they be blessed. Occasionally, you may actually pronounce a benediction, "God bless you." In so doing, you
are manifesting God's vision of abundant life and creating a world
of blessedness rather than cursing. You will have an opportunity to
create an ecology of blessing whether you are at the workplace, the
checkout stand, taking the kids to afterschool activities, greeting
your spouse, or tucking your children in bed at night.

Second, explore the healing of memories. Pioneered by the
healing work of Matthew and Dennis Linn, my approach to the
healing of memories involves going back to a place in childhood
when you experienced pain or limitation. Begin by taking a few
minutes in quiet prayer, asking Jesus to be your healing companion
as you explore the past. Remember that you are not alone: if you
ascend to the heights, Jesus is there; if you descend to the depths,
Jesus is there also. Also, remember that if you uncover a particularly
painful memory, seeking the services of a trained therapist, pastor,
or spiritual guide can assist in the healing process.

After a time of stillness and prayer, invite Jesus to be companion on the journey. Ask him to help you explore a painful memory
from the past. When you have unearthed a memory, visualize the
scene, the characters, the event, and your response. Experience
your pain in that situation and its impact on your life. Visualize
Jesus as seeing through your eyes and feeling the pain that you are
experiencing. After a few minutes, experience Jesus taking on your
pain, lifting the burden from you, and enabling you to go forward
healed and whole. What is it like to be free from the weight of the

emotional and relational burdens of the past? Conclude by thanking God for His healing presence in your painful memory and in your journey ahead.

If you experience the painfulness of the same memory at a later time, take a moment to breathe deeply and imagine that Jesus is with you, carrying your load, surrounding you in a circle of love, and guiding you safely to the future.

Third, we can also heal our imagination and sense of possibilities, unleashing God's vision for us. Many of our limitations are self-imposed, and initially emerged through childhood experiences. While we need to be realistic about gifts and possibilities, realism does not preclude growth, new possibilities, and personal healing. As the apostle Paul said to the Philippians, "I can do all things through Christ who strengthens me." In Jesus' words to the man whose son was suffering from spirit possession, or epilepsy, "all things can be done" or "all things are possible for the one who believes." When God wants us to have abundant life, there is no reason to think small or limit God's vision for us.

In this healing practice, begin once more in quiet prayer, silently awakening to God's presence in your life. Reflect on an area of limitation with the following questions:

» What is the nature of the limitation? Is it environmental? Economic? Situational, and more or less out of your control?
» Is the limitation self-imposed? If so, what is its origin? (For example, a lovely friend of mine sees herself as "plain and unattractive" because of her father's constant badgering her about her weight as a child? Another friend was told he couldn't draw, so as an adult he refused to draw anything other than stick figures, until he took an adult education course and discovered he was a talented water color painter!)
» How have you responded to the limitation?
» How would your life change if you chose to live by possibility rather than limitation?

After this time of self-examination, once more take a few minutes for silent prayer, asking Jesus to be your companion and healer. Visualize Jesus sitting or standing beside you. Enter into a dialogue about your area of limitation with him. What does he say to you? What images of hope does he give you? Visualize Jesus telling you that "you can do all things." Now imagine yourself breaking free of your limitation and living a life of surprising possibility. See yourself living God's vision of possibility for you. Conclude with a prayer of gratitude and a petition for courage to take the next steps in living your possibilities.

Our visions need to be acted upon. In some small way, take the first steps activity in living out your possibility or possibilities. This may mean: enrolling in a class, making a phone call, reaching out to a friend, or exploring a new talent without fear of failure. Remember that God is blessing your journey and wants you to experience abundant life.

CHAPTER TEN

A LIFESTYLE OF HEALING

The apostles gathered around Jesus, and told him all that they had done and taught. [31] He said to them, "Come away to a deserted place all by yourselves and rest a while." For many were coming and going, and they had no leisure even to eat. [32] And they went away in the boat to a deserted place by themselves. [33] Now many saw them going and recognized them, and they hurried there on foot from all the towns and arrived ahead of them. [34] As he went ashore, he saw a great crowd; and he had compassion for them, because they were like sheep without a shepherd; and he began to teach them many things. [35] When it grew late, his disciples came to him and said, "This is a deserted place, and the hour is now very late; [36] send them away so that they may go into the surrounding country and villages and buy something for themselves to eat." [37] But he answered them, "You give them something to eat." They said to him, "Are we to go and buy two hundred denarii worth of bread, and give it to them to eat?" [38] And he said to them, "How many loaves have you? Go and see." When they had found out, they said, "Five, and two fish." ... [and five thousand were fed] [45] Immediately he made his disciples get into the boat and go on ahead to the other side, to Bethsaida, while he dismissed the crowd. [46] After saying farewell to them, he went up on the mountain to pray. – Mark 6:30-46

Running on Plenty. My good friend and colleague Suzanne Schmidt has written a book on professional wellness, entitled, *Running on Plenty at Work*.[1] I think that this is an apt description of how we should live our lives as followers of Jesus. Jesus came to

---

1 Suzanne Adele Schmidt and Krista Kurth, *Running on Plenty at Work* (Washington DC: Renewal Resources Press, 2003).

awaken us to abundant life characterized by health, energy, and insight that enlivens mind, body, spirit, relationships, and political and social involvement.

Yet, many of us are running on empty. We live by scarcity, believing we lack the time, talent, treasure, and energy to respond creatively to the ongoing challenges and possibilities of life. I recall a conversation with a young pastor, recently out of seminary and now leading her first congregation in Southern California: "I feel like I'm chasing my tail all day long. I'm so busy between sermon preparation, church meetings, figuring out the budget, and making calls that I hardly have time to study or pray. I'm also trying to be a good mother and wife, and spend quality time with my family. I feel like I never have enough time, and I'm always running behind!" Her sentiments were echoed by an active business person in the Central Pennsylvania community where I live: "Some days, I wish I could leave it all behind. I feel constantly on the run and stressed out. It's always one thing after another, and nothing's ever finished. I remember growing up in the fifties. We had a real Sunday here in Lancaster, where I grew up. The stores were closed, we went to church, had a roast for dinner, and played the rest of the day. I recall my mom and dad taking us on walks and then stopping by the filling station to get soda pop. Then, dad took a nap with the newspaper covering his face. I can still remember him snoring! I wish I could have more Sundays like that! Nowadays, I receive e-mails and text messages 24/7 and if I don't respond immediately, my customers will go somewhere else." While we may not be able to go back to bucolic Mayberry of the 1950's, we may be able to recover Sabbath time and take occasional sabbaticals from Facebook, the internet, and our iPhones!

Perspective is Everything. Mark 6:30-46 contrasts abundance and scarcity in our personal and professional lives. The disciples have just graduated from the "Jesus School of Theology and Ministry" and then are sent out on their own, two by two, to teach, preach, and heal. Jesus requires them to have companions in ministry, not only for the sake of accountability, but to lighten the load and give each one an opportunity for a little down time. While Mark's narrative may be theological rather than chronological, the gospel writer implies that during his disciples' preaching and healing mission, Jesus' cousin, spiritual companion, and intimate colleague John the Baptist is killed by Herod. Jesus is most likely grieving the loss of his dear companion and colleague when the disciples return, elated at their successes, yet completely worn out. Success breeds success, and this means greater demand on the disciples' time and energy. People begin to seek out the disciples as well as their teacher Jesus for healing and spiritual counsel. As Mark notes, "many were coming and going, and they had no leisure even to eat." What a curious line to be included in the gospels! But, it is obviously important to Mark to give an account of the stresses the disciples faced, and Jesus' response to their fatigue and potential burnout. The Christian communities to which Mark wrote may have been overwhelmed by the demands of sustaining new communities of faith, sharing the good news in the broader community, and supporting their families. They may have needed a model of healthy ministry that combined hard work, commitment, and spiritual renewal.

The story states that everyone is looking for the disciples. The needs are great and almost impossible for a small group to fill. They could teach and heal all day long without making a dent in responding to the spiritual and physical needs of the larger community. The stresses of life are not just the province of ministry, but everyday life. Tom and Susan, a professional couple with two young children confided in me, "We never get a moment to breathe. Each morning we race to take the kids to daycare and then to work. In the afternoon we race home to dinner, baths, and bedtime, and then sometimes we have to go online or make calls to finish our work, or prepare for tomorrow. Even weekends are filled with activities and catch up. We need a Sabbath. We need a spiritual getaway to pray, rest, and play with the kids. And, we need some time for ourselves as individuals and as a couple."

In the passage from Mark 6, Jesus does something counter intuitive. Instead of getting caught up in the urgency of peoples' unending needs, he invites his disciples to go "to a deserted place by themselves." Jesus knew that if they were continue to respond with compassion to peoples' pressing needs, they needed to take care of their own needs as well. They needed to reconnect with their inner resources – the wellspring of energy, creativity, and compassion. We don't know how long this retreat took, but I suspect they had a good meal, shared some stories, took a nap, and spent some time in prayer and meditation. Jesus knew that good ministry and healthy living requires a rhythm of rest and activity, and contemplation and action.

Contemplation and Compassion. Our retreats can't last forever. A crowd awaits Jesus and his companions as they near the lake shore. While there are days in which the needs of others – our children, parents, co-workers, colleagues, and vulnerable people – can become sources of stress and annoyance, the spiritually-renewed Jesus' first response to the crowds and their demand for his time and energy was hospitality and care. As the scripture says, "he had compassion for them, because they were like sheep without a shepherd."

Recently, psychologists have identified compassion fatigue and the burnout that often precedes it as occupational hazards among caregivers (pastors, nurses, doctors, social workers, lawyers, emergency workers, and even parents and the children of elderly adults). Emotionally overwhelmed by the depth and enormity of suffering they are experiencing, caregivers often shut down relationally and spiritually. They lose energy, optimism, and empathy. They go through the motions of caring, but their heart is no longer in it. Compassion fatigue and burnout are the "shadow side" of intimacy and care, whether for congregants, elderly parents, vulnerable patients, or dependent children. Without constant replenishment of our emotional and spiritual reserves, we are likely to lose heart and become alienated from those we are intended to support. Healers need healing, too!

Despite his work load, and constant demands on his time and energy, Jesus returns to preach, teach, and heal with energy and zest. Anxiety and burnout limits our sense of possibility. The world often shrinks to the size of our particular challenge, and often small challenges become great mountains. In this case, the challenge was feeding a crowd of several thousand women and men with few resources at their disposal. While the mechanics of this miracle will always be a mystery, one thing is clear: the crowd was fed as a result of Jesus' ability to see resources within the limitations of the situation. Just as he intuited a great school of fish, and then pointed Peter toward the bounty that awaited him (Luke 5:1-11), here Jesus recognizes that although five loaves and two fish cannot feed a multitude, a life of blessing and imagination can transform cells as well as souls and access the life-giving energy of the big bang and the power that moves the planets, stars, and galaxies.

Contemplation gives birth to imagination and the energy to bring forth possibilities out of the limitations of life. A lifestyle of healing – involving the interplay of action and contemplation and rest and work – opens us to God's ever-present healing energy and delivers us from the burdens of the moment. Surely this is what Jesus meant when he counseled his followers to "consider the lilies" (Matthew 6:25-34). When we recognize that we are always in God's care, we live by abundance rather than scarcity whether it applies to energy, economics, and time. No longer tyrannized by time, the urgency of others, or the disparity between our gifts and the needs of the world, we can respond creatively to the challenges of life.

The story ends with Jesus dismissing the crowd, sending his disciples ahead to the next destination, and going up on a mountain to pray, embodying the rhythm of contemplation and action that opened him to the unlimited energy of God.

Healing as Prevention. Although healing and forgiveness were at the heart of Jesus' message, a truly effective healing ministry centers on promoting health and well-being, as well as preventing illness. We can enhance the inner movements toward health and wholeness, embedded in our immune, circulatory, nervous, respiratory, and digestive systems by our spiritual and lifestyle practices. God's wisdom is revealed in the dynamic interdependence of body, mind, and spirit. Our body is the temple of God's spirit and worthy of our love and care. While Jesus never wrote a primer on physical, emotional, and spiritual well-being, his ministry points to a number of healing practices that can promote vitality, energy, and overall well-being.

First, *establish a creative and varied balance of rest and activity.* Good health requires the right blend of Mary and Martha, and contemplation and action. Jesus' ministry provides a model for a healthy professional and personal life. Jesus' definitely worked hard, but he also grounded his life in prayerfulness, light-hearted play, and celebrative meals. Although his mission was to share the good news of God's realm of Shalom and abundant life, he embodied the good news in a variety of ways: teaching, preaching, healing, conversation, table fellowship, time with children, and intimate friendships. Many scholars such as John Dominic Crossan see Jesus' open table as the incarnation of his ministry to nuisances and nobodies. But, that open table and radical hospitality was no doubt fun as well as educational and political.

Jesus regularly goes to deserted places to open up to God's guidance and energetic power (Mark 1:12-13:35-39). In like fashion, we can cultivate a rich and varied life, grounded in moments of prayer and meditation. Following our callings or vocations – and each of us has more than one – may lead us to learn new talents and open to a variety of tasks in the course of each day. These days, I have discovered that my primary mission is to bless, heal, and bring beauty to the earth. I live that out as a devoted husband, parent, and grandparent; faithful friend; creative writer, speaker, teacher, and pastor; homeowner; and public citizen. But, I weave all these activities together by twenty minute morning and afternoon prayer times involving a form of centering prayer, the use of biblical affirmations, and breath prayer between tasks.

A life committed to daily prayer enables us to see God's movements in every task of the day and our long term plans. It also enables us to live out our vocation despite the demands of our personal and professional lives. After a busy day of teaching, preaching, healing, and fellowship, Jesus goes to a lonely place to pray. His disciples hunt him down, filled with plans for his future. But, out of Jesus' centeredness in God, he maintains the course of his mission, not as a settled rabbi but as a healing teacher, and prophet of God's realm throughout the land (Mark 1:35-39).

Second, *take time for Sabbath.* Despite his conflicts with religious leaders over healing on the Sabbath, Jesus took the Sabbath seriously as a time of rest and rejuvenation. Jesus knew that he and disciples needed extended times for retreat and renewal. Today, many of us need to reclaim Sabbath as a spiritual practice. We may not be able to take a Saturday or Sunday Sabbath, especially if we're church workers. But, we can find a time each week to turn off the phone, drag ourselves away from the iPad, Kindle, or Nook, and close the door to our study or office. If we're a stay-at-home parent, we can find a caregiver, fellow parent, or relative to watch the children for a few hours or trade off child care with our spouse, partner, or friend.

Sue and Marti made a commitment to take a weekly Sabbath from the internet and business once they realize that they were always "on duty" with work and family. They decided to begin their Sabbath each Saturday at 3:00 p.m. after the family shopping and chores and one last look at their business mail were completed. Their Sabbath continued until dinner on Sunday evening, which always left them and their children a few hours to prepare for the week ahead. As Sue says, "We're not legalistic, but we recognized that we needed to stop for a day each week, take stock of our lives, and simply let go of our responsibilities to the wider world. If there's an emergency, we respond, but our goal is to be open to one another, our friends and family. I put my work phone aside and turn off my laptop and iPad. We spend time playing with our pre-teen children or going to museums, parks, or games. We set aside Sunday morning for church, and enjoy a leisurely afternoon, before having a casual dinner." Marti adds, "Sue and I try to give each other a few hours of individual Sabbath time each weekend. Usually, I take a few hours on Saturday morning at a local coffee house to read and enjoy a quiet latte, before doing the week's shopping. Then, for a few hours in the afternoon, I take over the responsibilities while Sue takes a long run or reads. We try to take a family hike when the weather's good." Both Sue and Marti assert that, despite taking extra time off, the week ahead seems more spacious and they feel more creative in their professional lives.

Third, *make prayer a priority.* The apostle Paul counseled, "Pray without ceasing" (1 Thessalonians 5:17). This was not for Paul, "one more thing to do," but an attitude of life in which all things, large and small, can be brought to God in petition, intercession, and thanksgiving. Sandy notes that her life was transformed when she began the practice of breathing her prayers. "I'm always on the go, between work, school, family, and the kid's activities. I used to get so wound up that I couldn't sleep at night. Now, throughout the day, I pause and take few deep breaths as I say to myself, 'I breathe the Holy Spirit deeply in.' When I exhale, I let go of the stresses of the moment. When I take time to breathe my prayers and it's now a habit, I feel like I have enough time and energy. I don't panic anymore; I breathe and let go."

Fourth, *learn to meditate.* Jesus went to lonely places for extended prayer or meditation. Herbert Benson describes the impact of meditation in terms of the "relaxation response." Whether we simply breathe in God's spirit or focus on a prayer word, times of silence not only awaken us to God's still small voice, they also refresh and rejuvenate our bodies. In contrast to the frantic pace of the "fight or flight response," the "relaxation response" lowers our blood pressure and steadies our breath; it also strengthens our immune system and decreases physical and emotional stress. Tabitha notes that "my daily meditation time – and I use 'spirit' as my prayer word – calms, relaxes, and energizes. I feel a deep and abiding peace that I bring to my work place and relationships. What's more, I've managed to lower my blood pressure through meditation, diet, and weight loss, and no longer need, according to my physician, to take medication for hypertension."

Fifth, *simplify your life.* That wonderful Shaker hymn proclaims, "It's gift to be simple. It's a gift to be free." Some of us are possessed by our possessions and addicted to our activities. We are constantly on alert, driven by adrenaline, caffeine, and urgency. We don't know what it is like simply to "sit there and do nothing" or to refrain from impulse buying or frenetic activity.

Have you ever noticed at the mall or work place how many people are constantly on their cell phones or walk around with "ear buds" as they listen to music? Now, I use a cell phone regularly, and I like music. But, I've discovered that being constantly on the go, doing, and accumulating, may lead to loneliness and isolation rather than the communication we crave through the use of text messaging and cell phone use. Tom experienced a wakeup call when his wife complained, "Tom, you're sitting next to me, but you're not here. Even when we're watching a movie, if your phone buzzes or iPad chimes, you go somewhere else. After a hard day at work, I need you and not a man with a machine." Tom confessed that initially it was "hard to go cold turkey for a few hours each night. But my life is so much more satisfying. I am here in the present moment, and that's really helped my marriage and parenting."

Sixth, *celebrate nutrition.* Jesus enjoyed eating. He was even accused of being a drunkard and glutton (Matthew 11:19). His eating wasn't just work-related or a way of welcoming the outcasts, marginalized, and neglected. Jesus delighted in companionship around the dinner table. When Jairus' daughter is awakened from a life-threatening coma, Jesus tells her family to make her a good meal. Jesus rejoiced in mealtimes spent with Mary, Martha, and Lazarus. You can imagine the delight of the crowd when they took the first bites of bread and fish. I suspect that they were fed in spirit as well as body and smacked their lips at Jesus' culinary achievement.

Rejoice in your meals. Give thanks for the bounty of the earth. Take time to discern the foods that make you feel good and also support your well-being. While there are many healthy diets, a good life involves balance – not too much and not too little –

and variety in vegetables, fruits, and depending on your personal choices and potential allergic conditions, meats and grains. The key is awareness. This isn't legalism, but the sheer enjoyment of food that is good for you: simple, unprocessed "soul" food rather than high-calorie and complex "fast food."

I have found that simplicity in eating is the key to better health. I must confess that I am heavier than I'd like to be. But, I am learning to be more mindful and self-aware. This means focusing on my eating and the taste of food, rather than seeing my meal as an adjunct to typing on the computer, talking on the cell phone, or working on a project. It also means practicing self-restraint. This is a challenge since my primary workplace is my home. Rather than grabbing a handful of nuts or chips as I pass through the kitchen, I need to remind myself that good health involves simplicity and that I can wait till lunch! I try to exercise even for just fifteen minutes, an hour after every meal. My goal is to eat and drink reasonably and joyfully, and give thanks for the bounties of the earth and the body God has given me.

Seven, *take your time.* Physician Larry Dossey states that one of the primary sources of illness in modern civilization is "time" or "hurry sickness." He believes that stress-related illness is often related to our perception of time as scarce and fleeting. We live by "deadlines" and "kill time" when healthy living calls us to "life lines" and rejoicing in this day that God has made. I have begun to change my language. For example, although I need to finish this book by June 1, 2012, I don't describe that date as a "deadline" – as if the world would come to an end if I'm a few days late! I say "lifeline" or "schedule" as a way of changing my attitude toward my tasks. Believe it or not, letting go of "deadlines" makes my work more fluid – I anticipate finishing this text by Ash Wednesday – three months early! I work hard as a speaker, pastor, teacher, and writer, but when I "consider the lilies," I discover that I always have enough time and energy for good work, friends, family, and rest.

Prayer changes things, and it also changes time. A saying attributed to the Protestant Reformer Martin Luther is: I have so much to do today, that I need to pray more. Many of us forget to pray or meditate when we're busy. But, prayer and meditation transform our experience of time – they slow down our perception of time and enable us to experience the everlasting amid temporality. We discover that the vision of everlasting life not only motivates us to a life of mission and love, but also a sense of peace about the passage of time and our ability to complete our tasks. Meditation helps us to experience each of our tasks as important but not all-important. In light of God's everlasting life, time is abundant and full and we will find fulfillment on our journeys.

Eight, *reach out to others.* Good health involves healthy relationships. Perhaps, you remember the medical studies involving infants who were touched only as necessary. Their health was at risk. As Genesis says, it is not good to be alone; we are made for relationship. Reaching out to others liberates us from the burden of isolation. Our joys and challenges are intended to be shared, whether by regular physical contact, e-mail and text messaging, and phone conversations.

Nine, *ask for help.* We live in an independent universe in which no one is self-made or ultimately isolated. The words of I Corinthians 12 present a vision of spiritual community, the body of Christ, in which our joys and sorrows are joined with one another. We cannot flourish in the body of Christ without the well-being of the other members. A curious passage from Exodus 18 demonstrates what happens when we think we can go it alone, solving our problems and running our business without the companionship of others.

> *The next day Moses sat as judge for the people, while the people stood around him from morning until evening. [14]When Moses' father-in-law saw all that he was doing for the people, he said, "What is this that you are doing for the people? Why do you sit alone, while all the people stand around you from morning until evening?" [15]Moses said to his father-in-law, "Because the people come to me to inquire of God. [16]When they have a dispute, they come to me and I decide between one person and another,*

and I make known to them the statutes and instructions of God."
[17]Moses' father-in-law said to him, "What you are doing is not
good. [18]You will surely wear yourself out, both you and these people
with you. For the task is too heavy for you; you cannot do it alone.
[19]Now listen to me. I will give you counsel, and God be with you!
You should represent the people before God, and you should bring
their cases before God; [20]teach them the statutes and instructions
and make known to them the way they are to go and the things
they are to do. [21]You should also look for able men among all the
people, men who fear God, are trustworthy, and hate dishonest
gain; set such men over them as officers over thousands, hundreds,
fifties and tens. [22]Let them sit as judges for the people at all times;
let them bring every important case to you, but decide every minor
case themselves. So it will be easier for you, and they will bear the
burden with you. [23]If you do this, and God so commands you, then
you will be able to endure, and all these people will go to their
home in peace." – vv. 18-22

I often tell my seminary students and pastors I mentor that
"ministry is a marathon and not a sprint." This applies to the lives
of laypeople as well. If we go it alone at breakneck speed, we will
soon wear out and burn out. We will lose the zest of life and the
sense of wonder and vision that makes each day an adventure. Jesus was not a rugged individualist. He sought the companionship
and support of a group of men and women with whom he would
ministry, share the good news, and enjoy friendship, celebration,
and table fellowship. Jesus did not begrudge the achievements of his
followers. In fact, he promised that they could do "greater things."
When Jesus sent his disciples out on their first mission, they went
out in pairs, no doubt, to support one another, to provide times
for rest, and to hold each other accountable.

Deborah hated to ask for help. She didn't even like to ask her
husband or family to help her out. But, when she found herself
over her head with the challenges of work, going back to school
to get her degree, and child care, she knew she had to reach out.
"I just never could ask for help. I felt it made me look weak, or

people would want something from me in return. If I did it on my own, I wouldn't have to owe anybody anything, even my husband. And, I knew it would be just right! But, to my amazement, my life was changed when I said the simple words, 'Can you help me?' I discovered that people cared, that they had no hidden agendas, or wanted something in return. Now I feel rested, and not so alone. Now, I feel like helping others when they reach out. My life is so much richer and I have better relationships just because I realized I could ask for help."

Ten, *use your imagination.* Jesus saw a crowd enjoying a meal as he gazed upon five loaves and two fish. He saw disciples and world-changers in a handful of women and men. He saw beloved children of God in the toddlers and children who wanted to play with him. He saw saints emerging from people who thought they were outcasts and sinners.

I recently received a note from a former student who had been diagnosed with breast cancer. I had shared with her some spiritual exercises to practice while she received chemotherapy. I had counseled her to see the chemotherapy in terms of God's heal-ing light flowing through her body and to perceive the medicine, despite its inconvenient side effects, as a healing balm and not an inconvenience. I also counseled her to practice the "encircling" or "caim" from Celtic spirituality. In the encircling prayer, a person does one of two things:

» Rotate slowly clockwise in a circle, pointing outward with your index finger, until you have inscribed a circle around yourself. As you rotate, pray for God to be your companion on your day's adventures.

» If you are bedridden or unable to draw a physical circle, visualize a circle of protection around you, as you pray for God's encircling care.

The prayer of encircling reminds us that wherever we are and whatever we are doing, we are in God's hands and that truly nothing can separate us from the love of God.

Healing is about prevention and faithfulness as well as responding to sickness and sin.

While mortality is our gift and destiny, and even the best practices of prevention cannot protect us from unexpected catastrophic illness, a life devoted to our well-being and the well-being of others will truly be joyful and energetic, regardless of life's circumstances.

HEALING MARKS

In this chapter, I will suggest two healing practices: self-examination regarding your use of time and centering prayer. Together, these practices will alert you to your current quality of life and attitude toward time and deepen your experience of God's healing presence.

Self-examination. Begin with a time of silence. Breathe gently and deeply as you withdraw from your daily activities in search of a wider perspective. Experience the spaciousness of everlasting life in the midst of time and your connectedness with God's enlivening power. Open yourself to the love in which you live and move and have your being.

Take some time to reflect on an average day in your life, guided by the following questions:

» How do I feel physically? Emotionally? Spirituality?
» Do you I feel at peace or rushed?
» Do I have a vision that guides my daily activities or do things simply happen to me or do I simply go from one task to another without a coherent sense of purpose?
» How do I spend the day and week in terms of time related to: Work? Significant relationships? Children? Friends? Prayer? Hobbies and avocations? Service to the church and

community? Do I feel comfortable how I am spending my time?

» Are there activities that I am neglecting as a result of my choices?
» What is the state of my prayer life? Quiet time for meditation?
» Do I view time in terms of possibilities or deadlines?
» How might I change my life to be more aligned with my values and God's vision for my life? What first steps might I take in this process of experiencing the time of my life in terms of God's everlasting life and my personal priorities?

Centering Prayer. Centering prayer is one of many forms of Christian meditation.[1] The practice is quite simple. The challenge is to make meditation or Centering Prayer central to your lifestyle and spiritual commitments.

First, find a comfortable position. This may be a straight chair, a recliner, a wing chair, or yoga-style on the floor or a rug. Close your eyes and begin to breathe gently and peacefully. After a moment or two, ask for God's healing and enlivening presence to enlighten, guide, and transform you.

Second, focus your mind on a particular prayer word such as: joy, love, peace, Christ, Spirit, holy, or any other word that is both simple and meaningful. My own centering phrase is "God's light." As I inhale, I say silently "God's" and as I exhale, I say silently "Light" as I breathe God's light into the world. Focus fifteen to twenty minutes on your prayer word as a pathway to experiencing God's loving energy in your life. If your mind wanders, simply bring it back to your prayer word, without judgment or condemnation.

Conclude your time of meditation with a prayer for the day or the Lord's Prayer or some other meaningful prayer.

---

1 Thomas Keating, *Intimacy with God: An Introduction to Centering Prayer* (New York: Crossroads, 2009).

CHAPTER ELEVEN

HEALING IN A PLURALISTIC AGE

John said to him, "Teacher, we saw someone casting out de-mons in your name, and we tried to stop him, because he was not following us." [39]But Jesus said, "Do not stop him; for no one who does a deed of power in my name will be able soon afterwards to speak evil of me. [40]Whoever is not against us is for us. [41]For truly I tell you, whoever gives you a cup of water to drink because you bear the name of Christ will by no means lose the reward." – Mark 9:18-21

Faith, Medication, and Complementary Medicine. Alicia came to my study after church with serious questions involving the intersection of faith and medical care. Her children and husband had gone home in a separate car and she had an hour to talk to her pastor about her health condition. She confided, "I've been feeling very depressed lately. I have trouble getting out of bed, and just drift through the day. I'm not unhappy, exactly. I just don't have any motivation, the smallest thing is a great effort. I have to kick myself in the butt to get the kids off to school, cook dinner, and clean up. Then I collapse just as my husband comes home from work. I've been to see our family physician, and he referred me to a psychiatrist who wants me to take Prozac. But I'm resisting. I think as a Christian I ought to be able to get out of this funk on my own. If I have enough faith, won't I feel happy again? I feel like I'm failing God and my family if I have to resort to drugs to feel better."

We talked together for an hour and then took a stroll through the apple orchards that adjoined the church cemetery. She needed understanding and empathy, but she also needed permission to take a medication that might provide a cure for the depression that was immobilizing her.

As I pastor, my role is not to convince people to agree with my theological or political positions, but to raise provocative questions that help people connect their faith with their daily personal, communal, and political decision-making. I asked Alicia, "What would you do if you or your child had an ear infection? Wouldn't you take an antibiotic if the doctor prescribed it? Would that be letting God down? In what ways is your chemically-based depression any different than an ear infection or allergy attack?" Over the next few months, she chose to take medication; she also visited me on a bi-weekly basis for conversation and spiritual direction. Today, she is energetic and a happy witness to the interplay of what Dr. Dale Matthews calls the power of joining prayer and Prozac to bring healing and wholeness to our emotional lives.

Virtually every year, we read headlines that report the "negligence" of parents who depend on prayer to cure a sick child rather than going to the doctor. In almost every case, the parents of these children belong to churches that believe that faithful Christians should depend solely on the power of prayer rather than medicine to respond to illness. One parent confessed that "we decided not to take our son to the doctor because we knew that the prayers of a faithful person are always more effective than medications or surgery. We figured that if we had enough faith, our child would get well." Their statement about the effectiveness of medicine may have been true in the first century, when medical care often caused more harm than good, especially among middle and poor class of people. In those days, prayer and placebo effect – the impact of positive thinking on health – might have been the most helpful tools to respond to self-limiting illnesses and chronic conditions. Today, however, given advances in medical diagnosis and treatment, I believe Christians need to see God's presence in surgery and medicine as well as in prayer, faith, and positive thinking.

The rise of complementary medicine – and some studies say that over 50% of North Americans have used some form of complementary medical treatment - has also led to theological confusion among Christians. In a document released in May 2009, "Guidelines for Evaluating Reiki as an Alternative Treatment," the United States Council of Roman Catholic Bishops condemned reiki healing touch, a form of energy work popular among lay Christians and Roman Catholic women's religious orders, as superstitious, without support in Christian belief, unscientific, and inappropriate for Catholic institutions. The Bishops saw reiki healing touch, whose philosophical foundations are in many ways similar to acupuncture, Qigong, and other Chinese and Japanese energy therapies, as inappropriate for Christian use because it does not require Christian prayer and is handed down from the Reiki Master to her or his student. Sadly, the Bishops did not cite the growing number of medical centers that use reiki as a modality for stress reduction and pain relief, nor did they pay attention to the many anecdotal testimonies to the benefits of reiki in overall well-being and spiritual growth. While the research on the medical benefits of reiki is still inconclusive – as it is for most forms of complementary medicine – reiki is currently the subject a number of studies, sponsored by the National Institutes of Health. Moreover, the Roman Catholic Bishops falsely assumed that reiki was the sole province of new age healers and could not be integrated with Christian faith or contemporary Western medicine. Reiki is taught by many Christian ministers and laypeople as well as Roman Catholic nuns, for whom it is an important part of their self-care and pastoral practice. I mention the Bishops' pronouncement because: 1) its spirit is similar to the disciples' ostracism of the alternative healer mentioned in Mark and 2) it raises the question of what medical treatments are permissible for Christians. Further, as a result of my experience as a reiki master, teacher, and practitioner, I have experienced the health benefits of reiki in relieving toothaches, reducing stress, aiding in the healing of wounds and broken bones, and providing palliation for persons receiving chemotherapy, radiation, and hospice care.[1]

A Monopoly on Healing? Quite satisfied with their orthodoxy and ability to maintain the purity of Jesus' healing ministry,

---

1 See http://www.catholicnewsagency.com/news/bishops_new_guidelines_
condemn_reiki_therapy_as_superstition/. Last accessed October 30, 2012.

the disciples come to Jesus with what they assume is good news: "Teacher, we saw someone casting out demons in your name, and we tried to stop him, because he was not following us." They expect a pat on the back for maintaining decency, order, and clarity in Jesus' healing lineage. Imagine their surprise when the Healer retorts:

> *"Do not stop him; for no one who does a deed of power in my name will be able soon afterwards to speak evil of me. [40]Whoever is not against us is for us. [41]For truly I tell you, whoever gives you a cup of water to drink because you bear the name of Christ will by no means lose the reward." – Mark 9:39-41*

The one who opened the floodgates to divine healing and hospitality to all people by welcoming sinners, social outcasts, diseased women, lepers, tax collectors, foreigners, and persons possessed by demons, adds one more scandalous footnote to his healing ministry; divine healing is not restricted to his direct followers or even to Christians. God wants everyone to live abundantly and will use any healthy means to bring us to well-being.

"Whoever is not against us is for us," proclaims the healer Jesus. Anyone who aligns her or himself with God's realm of Shalom and healing, shares in Jesus' ministry of wholeness, without exception. Compassionate care cuts across denominational, theological, liturgical, and ethnic boundaries and includes seekers, doubters, and persons from other religious traditions. This is truly good news for persons in need. Jesus' ministry inspired early Christian theologians whose affirmation of the wisdom of Greek philosophers and the Jewish tradition, led them to assert that wherever truth is present, God is its source. In this passage, Jesus' message suggests a further theological insight: wherever truth and healing are present, God not only is its source but calls us, when appropriate, to embrace non-Christian forms of healing. This universalistic understanding of healing allowed early Christians to embrace the healing techniques of Hippocrates and Greek medicine, the Gentile forerunners of Western technological medicine. Later, it served to inspire Christians to create hospices for sick pilgrims and become leaders in the development of Western medicine through the founding of hospitals. Despite the fact that the current practice of Western medicine seeks to transcend any narrow religious tradition, including Christianity, most Christians today see no conflict between attending worship and taking medication or having surgery.

From this perspective, God is at work in "secular" medicine, even when Jesus' name is not invoked. Few physicians invoke God in their treatment plans or counsel their patients to go to healing services; rather they prescribe medications, surgery, and other forms of therapy. Still, I believe that God is inspiring and guiding physicians, nurses, technicians, and researchers, whether they are Jews, Muslims, Hindus, Buddhists, agnostics, or atheists, and is as present in the operating theatre as well the congregational healing service.

Good News for Complementary Medicine. In many ways, while Jesus did not prescribe a particular technique, his style was similar to many of today's complementary medical care givers. Jesus asked questions related to peoples' spiritual lives. He also touched them, nurtured their sense of hope and optimism, invited them to see their illness as part of a larger tapestry of life, challenged them to become active rather than passive in responding to illness, and invited them to experience the Holy One through prayer, faith, and trust. Moreover, Jesus used traditional healing remedies such as mud poultices and spittle to mediate and enhance God's healing power. Jesus also appears to have been a conduit of divine energy: when the woman with the flow of blood touched Jesus, her faith was met with a burst of energy not unlike the *ki* or *chi* described by traditional Japanese and Chinese medicine.

Like many complementary healers today, Jesus addressed the spiritual as well as physical aspects of health and illness, and elicited the inner resources of persons in partnership with God's vision of personal and global healing. To the paralyzed man at the pool, Jesus inquired: "Do you want to be made well?" To sight-impaired Bartimaeus, Jesus asks, "What do you want me to do for you?" As a model for today's complementary healers, Jesus invited agency rather than passivity in the healing process.

In contrast to those who see the soul as separate from and superior to the body, Jesus affirmed a mind-body-spirit unity. Our faith can shape our physical condition. Conversely, our physical condition can influence our emotional and spiritual lives and place in the social order. Touch can transform our emotional lives and forgiveness can promote physical recovery.

When John's Gospel asserts that "true light, which enlightens everyone, was coming into the world" (John 1:9), his affirmation opens the door to healers of all kinds. While Christians must be judicious in their use of complementary as well as technological medicine, there is nothing to hinder Christians from using any technique that reduces suffering and restores well-being to vulnerable people.

In contrast to the Roman Catholic Bishops' pronouncements, I believe that Christians can use and modify non-Christian practices such as reiki, Qigong, acupuncture, and yoga for promoting well-being and addressing issues of pain, stress, and overall well-being. There is a point of contact between the scalpel, the apothecary, the healing touch, and Jesus' healing ministry. For over twenty-five years, I have been a practitioner of reiki healing touch. For nearly twenty years, I have been a reiki teacher/master whose primary focus is building a bridge between Christian faith and reiki healing touch. I regularly teach reiki courses to pastors and laypeople, and have provided theological, spiritual, and practical guidance for congregations seeking to initiate healing ministries, involving laying on of hands in worship along with reiki healing touch.

When I practice reiki, I place my hands on my partner's body as I open to the divine healing energy in whom we live and move and have our being. I invoke God's presence asking that God move through my hands to bring healing to others. I place my hands at various parts of my partner's body, mediating *ki* or *chi*, an energy similar to the power that flowed from Jesus to heal the woman with a flow of blood. I assume that I am sharing in God's vision of healing and abundant life whether I am giving a reiki treatment, leading a healing service involving laying on of hands, or praying for someone in person or from a distance. Although God is the ultimate source of healing, techniques like reiki, healing worship, intercessory and petitionary prayer, acupuncture, and yoga open us to greater influxes of divine energy. Accordingly, I see reiki healing touch and other complementary healing modalities as appropriate partners with prayer, meditation, and Western medical care. From my perspective as a follower of Jesus, the use of reiki is no more foreign to Christian faith than my recent use of antibiotics to treat bronchitis, my regular use of medications to control hypertension, or my best friend's use of chemotherapy and radiation in response to cancer.

The healing power of Jesus, as Mark 9:18-21 indicates, is larger than Christianity and inspires Jesus' followers to employ any technique that reduces human suffering. My use of reiki healing touch has given me greater insights into Jesus' healing ministry and my vocation as healing companion to vulnerable people. A good friend of mine, an active Roman Catholic, has found yoga and Tai Chi complementary to her participation in worship and her daily practice of centering prayer.

Guidelines for Christians. The first principle of medicine and theology alike is first to do no harm. In the course of this text, we have already explored theological viewpoints that blame the victim, assert that illness is the result of God's will or God's punishment for sin and disobedience, and encourage passivity rather than agency in seeking our own well-being and the well-being of others. These are all explanations that stand in the way of discovering God's care for the sick and the meaning of Jesus' healing ministry for persons today.

The primary responsibility of persons who seek to integrate complementary medicine with Christian faith is, first of all, to pray for God's guidance. As scripture says, "ask and it will be given to you; search and you shall find; knock, and the door will be opened for you" (Matthew 7:7). Ask God if reiki, therapeutic touch, healing touch, or another complementary modality is a spiritual path you should take in the healing process of others or yourself. Take time to listen to God's wisdom in intuitions, chance encounters, dreams, and words of guidance.

Second, seek out Christians who are practicing particular complementary medical techniques. Enter into dialogue with pastors and complementary and Western health care professionals to discern how they integrate their faith in Christ with the use of non-Western practices.

Third, seek out a spiritual guide who has some knowledge of the broad spectrum of Western and complementary medical practices along with a concern for Jesus' healing ministry and the healing ministry of the church. In the spirit of young Jesus, who conversed with the rabbis at the Jerusalem temple, take time for dialogue and discernment, with the questions: "Is this a spiritual path for me? How will it deepen my commitment to healing prayer? Do I experience God's presence in this spiritual practice?" Give yourself time for the answers to emerge, recognizing that God's vision for your life is unique and may differ from other Christians.

Fourth, do your homework. Learn about the philosophical and spiritual foundations of complementary medical practices. Are they congruent with your understanding of Jesus' healing ministry? Do they respond to health and sickness in ways that console vulnerable people and those who fail to improve despite their use of complementary medicine? Is there a sense of grace in the theology and treatment?

Fifth, seek out complementary health teachers who are known for their integrity and sensitivity to the insights and wisdom of Christian faith. While you can benefit from physicians and complementary practitioners who are not Christians, I believe that it is important to study with people who have an awareness and affirmation of your deepest spiritual values and are committed to your spiritual path as a Christian. This counsel is true whether you are seeing a medical doctor, counselor, clinical social worker, psychiatrist, or complementary care giver. Similar to the healing of Jairus' daughter, we need people who not only challenge us but understand and support us to experience healing and wholeness.

Sixth, look for other Christians who are also practicing the technique that interests you. In many communities, there are small groups that gather, often in churches, for healing touch, reiki, therapeutic touch, Qigong, and yoga. These groups will give you an opportunity to learn from each other, grow in faith together, and hold each other accountable to the highest ethical and spiritual values.

Seventh, let go of results either of prayer, healing worship, and complementary health care. Too often televangelists and complementary healers claim to know what is best for persons suffering from illnesses of body, mind, and spirit. They assume to know the meaning of healing for every individual. They also judge people who don't get well despite their ministrations. Whether practicing liturgical laying on of hands in a church service or reiki healing touch at a healing center, congregational parlor, or hospital room, your role is simply to be God's healing companion, letting God's love flow through you in a unique and supportive way. Praying with our hands in safe and welcome ways is one of the greatest gifts we can give another, regardless of the results. Remember, even when there cannot be a cure, there can always be a healing. As pastor Rob Bell asserts, "Love wins." Whether we live or die we are in God's care and nothing can ever separate us from the love of God in Jesus Christ our healer (Romans 14:8; Romans 8:38-39).

Finally, and here I am going to repeat myself because our relationship with God'a abundant life and love is the key to healing and wholeness: saturate everything you do with prayer in Jesus' name. Names have power and Jesus' name can still the storms and energize our spirits. Invoking Jesus the Christ places us in a circle of wisdom, protection, and healing. Let Jesus' hands guide your healing touch. Open to Jesus' healing energy as you seek to minister to others. Awaken to the holy energy that flowed from Jesus to the woman who suffered from bleeding. Surround yourself with God's ever-present guidance and protection in settings where you are praying with your hands, asking only and always to be a channel of God's love.

HEALING MARKS

Whether or not you ever explore a complementary or non-Christian healing practice, you can experience the energy that gave birth to the universe, brought forth planets and humankind, and courses through your cells as well as your spirit.

In this healing practice, begin with a time of quiet prayer, guided by the words of the gospels: "true light, which enlightens everyone, was coming into the world" (John 1:9), and "you are the light of the world.... let your light shine" (Matthew 5:13-16).

Breathe deeply allowing each breath to calm and ground you in God's healing presence. After a few minutes, visualize each breath as filled with healing light, entering your body, filling it from head to toe, cleansing and healing any disease, calming any stress, refreshing any weariness. Bathe yourself in God's healing light, experiencing divine healing, saturating every cell and then surrounding you with comfort and protection.

Filled with God's presence, take a moment to visualize an intimate friend or family member. Visualize the two of you joined by God's light. Experience your connectedness, allowing the healing energy you are experiencing to flow into their lives in a supportive way. Visualize them as healthy and whole in God's presence.

Still, filled with God's presence, take a moment to visualize someone whom you perceive in need of God's healing touch. Visualize the two of you joined by God's light. Experience your connectedness, allowing the healing energy you are experiencing to flow into their lives in a supportive way. Visualize them as healthy and whole in God's presence.

Return to your breath, simply dwelling in the joyful companion of God's healing light. After a few minutes, take some time to give thanks for God's love and the light that fills your life.

CHAPTER TWELVE

AN EMPTY TOMB AND AN OPEN FUTURE

When the Sabbath was over, Mary Magdalene, and Mary the mother of James, and Salome bought spices, so that they might go and anoint him. ²And very early on the first day of the week, when the sun had risen, they went to the tomb. ³They had been saying to one another, "Who will roll away the stone for us from the entrance to the tomb?" ⁴When they looked up, they saw that the stone, which was very large, had already been rolled back. ⁵As they entered the tomb, they saw a young man, dressed in a white robe, sitting on the right side; and they were alarmed. ⁶But he said to them, "Do not be alarmed; you are looking for Jesus of Nazareth, who was crucified. He has been raised; he is not here. Look, there is the place they laid him. ⁷But go, tell his disciples and Peter that he is going ahead of you to Galilee; there you will see him, just as he told you." ⁸So they went out and fled from the tomb, for terror and amazement had seized them; and they said nothing to anyone, for they were afraid. – Mark 16:1-8

Surrounded by Death. As I write these words, one of our dear friends, Carol, is in hospice care, facing her final weeks of life. I have known Carol for thirty years. We met as next door neighbors and parents of our toddlers, who still remain best friends. We've shared countless meals, trips to Turtle Park in Northwest Washington DC, and conversations about the spiritual journey. A few years ago, Carol was diagnosed with colon cancer. Initially, this spirit-centered woman in her mid-seventies fought the good fight with chemotherapy and the best Western medical care possible. A deeply spiritual Roman Catholic, she also continued practicing centering prayer, reading devotional literature, receiving reiki healing touch treatments from my wife, and intercessions from persons throughout the world. A few months ago, Carol decided that the physical side effects outweighed the few extra months she would receive from another round of chemotherapy. She is at peace, knowing that whether she lives or dies, she dwells in God's everlasting care.

As my wife and I prayerfully companion Carol and her family in this time of transition, I also daily intercede on behalf of my best friend and spiritual companion, diagnosed three years ago with lymphoma and what is described as incurable breast cancer. She, too, is a person of deep spiritual faith. She has a spirit of equanimity as she seeks to live long enough to see her young adult children launch out on their own as self-sufficient adults. I pray daily for her, interceding for her, surrounding her in light, and – in a behavior that may seem odd for a progressive Christian – rebuking the spirit of cancer. I send that spirit of illness into God's care to transform it into something of beauty. Still, her future is uncertain, especially as new cancerous lumps have been found in her neck. I can't imagine a world without my friend. I pray that we will grow old alongside one another as the best of spiritual friends. Yet, I know that her long-term health condition is uncertain.

Death is all round us. New pastors are often surprised to discover how much of ministry is defined by death and grief. Despite our advances in medical technology and crisis care, the mortality rate will remain at 100%. Longevity can never be confused with immortality. Even if we advance human life to one hundred and fifty years, as some futurists predict, we will eventually die of something. As C.S. Lewis asserts in his memoir on bereavement, *A Grief Observed,* grief is a necessary season of every good marriage. The cost of falling in love and living a wonderful life together as a couple is standing at the graveside or mourning at the memorial service, for the spouse that survives. Lewis waivers about whether Jesus did Mary, Martha, and Lazarus any favors: he had to die twice!

Yes, as Luther says, "in the midst of life we are surrounded by death," whether it be our own mortality, death from accident, natural disaster, or war, or incurable disease. Our responsibility as Christians is to fight for life at every front – by prayer, insuring universal medical care, eliminating dietary and environmental toxins, feeding and housing the hungry, and working for a sustainable and just peace. This is what it means to be God's companion in healing the world. But it is clear that while we may eliminate certain types of death – contagious diseases, starvation, cancer, AIDS – we can never eliminate the sting of death altogether. We struggle with the reality of death, physically, emotionally, and spiritually. Beyond that, we recognize with Martin Luther King that while longevity is important, it isn't the highest value compared to fidelity to God's reign of Shalom. We need a resurrection to have courage in this life and hope for the future.

Mark's Vision of Resurrection. Virtually every biblical scholar believes two things about the Gospel of Mark: 1) Mark is the earliest written gospel and 2) the original version of Mark concludes at Mark 16:8. The post-resurrection encounters of Jesus with the disciples, found in verses 9-20, are considered a later edition to the text. Having said this, we must remember that Christian faith is grounded in the surprising and unexpected resurrection of Jesus and that the apostle Paul's First Letter to the Corinthians, written perhaps a decade before Mark, affirms the reality of the resurrection (I Corinthians 15:1-58). Paul's life-changing words point to the significance of resurrection in shaping Jesus' first followers hopes, ethics, and lifestyle:

> *Death has been swallowed up in victory.*
> *Where, O Death, is your victory?*
> *Where, O Death, is your sting?* – *I Corinthians 15:54b-55*

Out of his resurrection hope, Paul could proclaim in Romans that "in all these things we are more than conquerors through him who loved us....[nothing in all creation] will be able to separate us from the love of God in Christ Jesus our Lord" (Romans 8:37, 39b).

Mark's resurrection account can be disappointing to people who want to know with certainty the architecture of heaven and the floor plans and interior design of its many mansions. According to most biblical scholars, Mark's version of the resurrection ends at verse 8, with a description of the women's response to the empty tomb: "So they went out and fled from the tomb, for terror and amazement had seized them; and they said nothing to anyone, for they were afraid." Eventually, however, the word got out, "Christ is not in the tomb. He is going ahead of you to Galilee, there you will see him."

Despite the brevity and apparent incompleteness of its resurrection narrative, Mark's gospel describes the interplay of death and hope. As they walked toward the tomb that first Easter, the disheartened women – Mary of Magdala, Mary the mother of James, and Salome – talk among themselves about what they would find at the tomb. Their first concern is accessibility. They witnessed the stone being placed at the entrance of the tomb (Mark 15:42-47). They want to show one last act of love for their teacher, healer, and friend, but their path to the future is blocked. "Who will roll away the stone for us from the entrance to the tomb?"

Their question is repeated in countless chemotherapy labs, hospital rooms, and in quiet moments when darkness encompasses us. "Who will roll away the stone of cancer? How will I face the future, not knowing whether I'll live or die? What will happen to my family after I'm gone?" As I noted earlier, when I heard that my son had a large mass in his chest, my visceral response was "he's going to die." In the first weeks of his treatment, I couldn't muster the sort of prayer I was used to saying in public places – a flowery address to God enumerating our needs and challenges. All I could say was, "Lord have mercy, Christ have mercy," as I walked the grounds of the university adjoining the hospital. My vision of the future was initially to just get him and his wife through this and provide comfort for my wife.

After the shock subsided, I discovered with the women that the stone of hopelessness had been rolled away. I mustered my imagination, energy, and hopefulness and got down to the hard work of helping him get well – through companionship, shedding tears with him, reporting his needs to the nurses and doctors, gathering a global prayer team, and walking to and fro with him to chemotherapy treatments and doctor's appointments. My prayers were punctuated by another prayer hymn, "Great is thy Faithfulness."

> Great is Thy faithfulness!
> Great is Thy faithfulness!
> Morning by morning new mercies I see
> All I have needed Thy hand hath provided
> Great is Thy faithfulness, Lord unto me![1]

"Who will roll the stone away" that bars the path to the future? Who will awaken our imagination and hope again? How will we live with an incurable illness and yet day by day reach out to others in love and service? That was the challenge for the three women when their world collapsed with Jesus' death and that is our challenge when we hear the dreaded words, "cancer," "ALS," "stroke," and "AIDS," for ourselves or a loved one.

Mark is no sickness-and-death-denying Pollyanna.[2] His resurrection account does not deny its mystery, unexpectedness, and open-endedness. Meeting an angel and receiving a mission from a spiritual being doesn't solve our problems. In fact, keeping hope alive at the bedside and maintaining a vision of the eternal when your beloved's life force is ebbing away with every tick of the clock can be a monumental task – the gift of grace and grit, and a village of loving and praying friends.

In the midst of helplessness and hopelessness, these courageous women – and they are courageous because they alone among Jesus' followers come to the tomb with all their fears, grief, and

---

1 Thomas Chisholm, "Great is Thy Faithfulness." (Some contemporary versions substitute "God" for "Lord.")
2 Perhaps the original Pollyanna wasn't Pollyannaish either: her "glad game" involved looking for something positive in every event, even negative ones. She may have discovered through the wisdom of her father that "in all things God is working for good," despite our current challenges.

hopelessness – receive a word that astounds them and takes awhile to sink in, "He is not here….he is going ahead of you." To their amazement, there is no corpse, but the message that Christ is alive, not bound by life or death, and will be with them in the future.

John's Gospel tells the story of Mary of Magdala in the garden. She comes in all her grief, and encounters a stranger whom she mistakes for the gardener. She implores him to tell her where Jesus' corpse may be found. It is then that she hears the stranger call out her name, "Mary," in a familiar voice that awakens her spirit and restores her to life. When she tries to hold onto the Risen One, he resists. "Do not hold onto me." He can no longer be confined to this body or to our previous understandings of who Jesus is. He is more than we can imagine, but he will be with us in every future that lies ahead.

Mark's original manuscript ends inconclusively at verse 8: the women are bewildered and remain silent. Eventually, however, the shock of resurrection subsides. Though it is not noted in Mark's text, we can imagine that once their experience in all its wonder soaks in, they rush to the disciples with good news, "He is not here. He is going ahead of you. He is awaiting you in the future – along the seashore of Galilee."

While I am inspired by the post-resurrection narratives in Matthew, Luke, and John, I find Mark's inconclusive version the most edifying to me precisely because it reflects my experience of the future. We must live through Holy Saturday in all its stark hopelessness before we can experience the celebration of Easter. Easter itself – as Mark suggests – does not solve all our problems or deliver us from pain and death. But, with the reality of the empty tomb an open future and the promise burst forth, promising that even when we cannot receive a cure, there is a healing. Christ goes ahead of us to every future we can imagine. Christ will be with us on the road as our companion in every experience of joy and sorrow, and celebration and mourning. We can take solace that the future is open and that although the details remain a mystery, God's presence remains a certainty. The healing power of the resurrection is found in companionship and care, large enough to encompass our doubts, and not in any clarity that reveals the exact details of our personal or planetary futures.

Wounded yet Living. While Mark gives no details about the resurrection life or Jesus' post-resurrection appearance, John's gospel suggests that the resurrected Jesus is not known by his perfection, but his wounds (John 20:24-29). Grief over the loss of loved ones never fully ends. The pain of loss remains even after the healing of bereavement or coming to terms with our own mortality. Now and again, my eyes still mist up when I think of my mother, Loretta, my father, Everett, and my brother, Bill. I become reflective when I think of my dear friend Wendy, my erstwhile high school girlfriend and friend over forty years, who died just a year ago from brain cancer. How can such wonderful lives be snuffed out? How could such vibrancy disappear from the face of the earth?

But, death is the cost of being born and grief is the cost of having loved and been loved. This is as true for God as it is for us. God will not retreat from the pain of the world, the suffering born of love, nor should we. We do not need an unfeeling, distant God, for whom our pain is purely observational. We need an intimate, suffering, and celebrating God who sits mourning alongside us at the graveside and feels our fear as we face the abyss of nothingness. Jesus is wounded and heals us by his wounds and intimacy. Some think that the primary sign of God's perfection is emotional distance and freedom from the pain of the world – the vision of a God who experiences uncontaminated bliss. I contend that God's bliss embraces the pain of the world and that God transforms our tears into celebration by taking the pain into Godself fully, completely, and intimately. Our wounds are Jesus' wounds and by "his stripes," that is, his sharing in our trauma, bereavement, waywardness, and pain, "we are healed" (Isaiah 53:4-5).

In the Midst of Death, We are Surrounded by Life. In Madeleine L'Engle's *A Ring of Endless Light*, Vicki Austin is grief-stricken as she imagines her grandfather dying of acute leukemia. When she shares her concerns, he reflects on his own life and notes that his vocation in his final days, despite his frailty, is to pray for the world. He has lived well, making his life a witness to his faith. Now, as he looks toward his imminent death and experiences greater and greater lapses of memory and clarity, he is making his death a witness to God as well.

As a pastor, I have visited many people at the descending edges of life. Often I have left comforted by their sense of hopefulness, often edified by paranormal visions and dreams of the afterlife. They have experienced everlasting life in the midst of time. As their bodies wear down, their spirits are growing in stature. They can claim, with the hymn writer, "It is well with my soul." They know that beyond the failures of medicine to keep them alive, there is a greater healing, companionship with the living God.

The resurrected Jesus is going ahead of us. The One who shares our joy and sorrow in the present is our companion in every future we can imagine for ourselves and our loved ones. We don't need to know the dimensions of heaven to trust the glorious adventures that God has prepared for us. I think of the faithful witness of my father. Like so many other faithful Christians, his trust in God over a lifetime made it possible for him to have a sense of God's future in spite of debilitation, compromised intellect, and vulnerability.

My dad's experience of God's nearness was echoed by Steve, one of my father's contemporaries in the Baptist church. Ninety-five years of age, he was diagnosed with incurable cancer. He continued to walk and play golf as long as he was able. When he could no longer walk, his bedroom became a shrine of prayerfulness and friendship as he awaited a holy adventure in companionship with God. He believed in the resurrection. He was agnostic about what it would be like, but he confided that "it is more than I can ever imagine. I expect there will be work for me to do on the other side, and I will be part of a communion of saints with the people I've admired in this lifetime – maybe Martin Luther King and Dietrich Bonhoeffer and Gandhi."

The scriptures say very little about survival after death. But, a few things seem to be clear. God's heavenly realm will be a community in which joy and growth, praise and wonder, will define our experience. Salvation is never solitary, but always communal. The same applies to the afterlife – it will be more than we can imagine in terms of intimacy, innovation, and growth. Second, resurrection life embraces the whole person. While our resurrection bodies may not be literal flesh and bones, I believe that they will encompass mind, emotion, spirit, and relationships. We will be known by a type of spiritual embodiment, as Paul suggests in I Corinthians 15, that will be more lively and dynamic than our current physical states. I recall Morton Kelsey, one of the pioneers in reviving healing ministries in mainstream Christianity, musing about Jesus' resurrection body and comparing it to the energy described by quantum physics, embodied yet energetic and more than we can imagine from our earthly perspective. I believe that the mystical experiences and sense of unity we have in this lifetime on a sporadic basis will be a continuous reality inspiring to continued growth and adventure. God is omnipresent in our world, but sadly we are oblivious to the God-moments that shape our lives constantly. I believe that in the afterlife, all moments will be God-moments as we fulfill our identities through forgiveness, growth, and creativity.

From this perspective, the afterlife is not the opiate of the masses or a retreat from this world. Our goal is not to be "so heavenly minded that we are no earthly good." Rather, the deepest meaning of the afterlife – the infinite value of each person as God's beloved – inspires us to social concern, justice-seeking, and care for the earth. What we do in our earthly lives truly matters to God and our neighbors. Though this world will pass away, it is still loved and treasured by the one to whom all hearts are open and all desires known. If I might make bold to say – and here I am taking a leap – if our identity persists in the afterlife in communion with God, then we are creating one another's future life by what we do today. We are contributing to the identities of dynamic and eternal children of God, who will take these identities into God's realm of adventurous growth.

In the midst of death, we can live surrounded by life. The stone has been rolled away, the tomb is empty, and Christ goes ahead of us into the future. This is the healing we seek. The healing that transforms every day and awakens us to God's healing touch that transforms our tears into joy and our fears into courage.

HEALING MARKS

While we see in a mirror dimly, and never can encompass the future God envisions for us, we can imagine what heaven is like. Though we need to be humble in our imagination, we can visualize our dreams of the future.

As in the case of all of our exercises, we begin with a generous silence. Then, take a moment to read these words from John 20:21-22:

> *Jesus said to them again, "Peace be with you. As the Father has sent me, so I send you." *²²*When he had said this, he breathed on them and said to them, "Receive the Holy Spirit."*

Imagine Jesus breathing in and through you. Visualize the moment of your death. Where are you? Who is with you? As you take your last breath, what happens? Is there anyone to greet you? Visualize the scene of letting go of this life and awakening to the afterlife.

As you enter the heavenly realm, what do you notice? Is anyone there to greet you? Take time to visualize what heaven is like. Take time to notice any familiar people. Along the way, you encounter Jesus. What does he look like? What does he communicate to you? How do you respond? Perhaps, he asks, "Is there anyone you would like to see? Is there anyone you need to reconcile with?" How do you respond? If you have a desire to meet some people, what do you say to them? How do they respond to you?

Take some time to enjoy the heavenly community. As you conclude this meditation, give thanks to God who has prepared a place for you and who has given you a future and a hope.

INTERACTIVE GROUP SESSIONS

SESSION ONE

SPIRITUAL PRACTICE

Each session will begin with a spiritual practice, grounded in my belief that theology and spirituality are intimately related. Biblical literacy is a matter of spirituality as well as textual knowledge.

We begin with the simplest spiritual exercise, breath prayer. After an opening prayer, take time to be still in God's presence, breathing gently and regularly. Imagine the power of the Holy Spirit entering you with each breath. You may choose to say to yourself, "I breathe the Spirit deeply in with each breath." If your mind wanders, bring it back to focus without judgment. Take a few minutes to breathe deeply, experiencing your unity with God's Holy Spirit.

QUESTIONS

1) When you think of the word "healing" what comes to mind?
2) How do you understand the nature of scripture? Should we read the scripture literally, imaginatively, or with a critical mind?
3) What is your response to television healers? What do you know of them? What do you think of their programs?
4) What is your favorite or most meaningful healing story from the gospels? Why is this story meaningful to you? Do you think these stories are relevant to our lives today?
5) How do you understand the relationship between technological and complementary/alternative medicine? What is your experience with complementary/alternative medicine?
6) What is your experience with prayer? Answered and unanswered?

7) When have you experienced serious illness? Have you found God's presence in difficult times?

CLOSING PRAYER

Conclude with breath prayer and an opportunity to lift up prayers of intercession and petitition.

SESSION TWO

SPIRITUAL PRACTICE

German mystic Meister Eckhardt proclaims that "If the only prayer you make is thanksgiving, that will be sufficient." For what are you thankful today? Share your gratitude as a group. Conclude with a prayer of gratitude for the ability to gather for study and reflection on the healings of Jesus.

QUESTIONS

1) What is the relationship between faith and healing? Does faith insure healing? What impact does faith have on our well-being?
2) Do you believe that negative thinking causes illness? In what ways might negative thinking contribute to illness?
3) Take moment to read Mark 5:25-34, the story of the woman with the hemorrhage. What problems did she face in her society? What were the obstacles to her seeing Jesus? What do your think of her boldness? How did her faith shape the healing she experienced?
4) Considering the woman with the flow of blood. What is the impact of chronic illness in our culture? Are certain illnesses "unclean" in our current culture? How might we respond to the social meanings of illness?
5) How do you define the "power" that flowed forth from Jesus? What do you think of the author's comparison of this power with "ki," "chi," and "prana," non-Western understandings of energy?
6) Have you ever experienced something similar to Jairus, his wife, and the author in terms of your relationship with a sick child, friend, and relative?
7) Read Mark 5:21-24, 35-41. As you consider Jairus' daughter, do you think it matters if she were "dead" or sleeping?" What

do you think of Jesus' creation of a healing circle? Who would
you ask to be in your healing circle?

8)   How do you understand the meaning of miracles? Are miracles
violations of the laws of nature? Or reflections of a partnership
between God and the world, operating within normal causal
relationships?

CLOSING PRAYER

In this visualization exercise, imagine the following: You have
been in a deep coma. In your coma, you hear a voice saying, "Little
child, wake up." You open your eyes and see the face of Jesus. What
does he look like? How do you feel upon awakening?

You start to move around, and hear Jesus say to you, "What
would you like to eat?" How do you respond? What favorite food
would you like Jesus to prepare for you?

Conclude by giving thanks for God's loving presence in your
life and the gifts of God's abundance in food and drink.

SESSION THREE

SPIRITUAL PRACTICE

Reflect on John 9:1-7 in the spirit of *lectio divina*, or holy reading. Begin with the breath prayer, described in Session Three. Read the text twice, inviting participants to listen for the word, phrase, or image that "speaks" to them spiritually. Take five minutes to meditate on the text and the word, phrase, or image that emerges, exploring quietly its meaning in your life. Conclude with sharing your insights with your neighbor and then the whole group.

QUESTIONS

1) What explanations have you heard for the suffering people experience? How do you respond to these explanations?
2) What is God's role in the events of our lives? Does God determine everything in advance? Do you think God causes cancer, accidents, tsunami, and the death of children? Is there randomness and chance in the universe?
3) Do you think God feels our pain? Does our pain make a difference to God?
4) What do you think of the author's vision of health and illness as the result of many factors, some of which are out God's complete control? What do think of a God who cannot control everything, but must experience tragedy along with us?
5) What do you think of the author's understanding of God as the limited, but fully loving and caring power seeking healing and wholeness for all of us? What do you think of the idea that God's power is relational and contextual, working within our lives, rather than determining everything?
6) How do you respond to Jesus' comment to the man healed of paralysis: *"See, you have been made well! Do not sin anymore, so that nothing worse happens to you?"*

7) How do you understand Rick Warren's belief that God's "purpose for your life predates your conception. He planned it before you existed, *without your input?*" Do you agree?

8) What role do we have in our own healing and wholeness, as well as illness? Are we agents or passive in relationship to illness and God's activity in our lives?

CLOSING

Conclude with a time of intercession, lifting up your concerns for yourself and others.

SESSION FOUR

SPIRITUAL PRACTICE

Begin with a *lectio divina* exercise, meditating on Mark 2:1-12. Listen for the word, image, or phrase that speaks to you. Share your insights with your neighbor and the group.

QUESTIONS

1) What role does belief – placebo and nocebo effect – have in health and illness? What role does the mind play in health and illness?

2) What is the role of forgiveness and guilt in health and illness?

3) What are the obstacles that the four friends faced? What obstacles have you and others faced as you seek healing and wholeness?

4) What do you think about Mark's comment – "when Jesus saw their faith?" What is the role of our faith in the well-being of others? Do you think believe in healing on behalf of others? Is personal faith necessary for our healing to occur or can others' faith influence our health outcomes?

5) Reflect on the passage from James: "Are any among you sick? They should call for the elders of the church and have them pray over them, anointing them with oil in the name of the Lord. ^{15}The prayer of faith will save the sick, and the Lord will raise them up; and anyone who has committed sins will be forgiven. ^{16}Therefore confess your sins to one another, and pray for one another, so that you may be healed. The prayer of the righteous is powerful and effective" (James 5:14-16). In what ways is this passage a model for healing worship? What role do you think "confession" has in well-being and recovery from illness? How do you understand "the prayer of faith?" What role does "anointing" have in healing?

6) Where have you discovered "angels in boulders?" Do you think that God is working for good in all things, without determining all things?

CLOSING

If it seems appropriate for your group, take time to create a healing circle. Invite anyone who desires "laying on of hands" to enter the center of the circle for healing prayer. You may choose to pray extemporaneously or use a prayer such as:

» We lay hands on you in the name of Jesus Christ that you may experience God's healing
» Touch for yourself and those for whom you pray.

Conclude this time with a prayer for healing for your congregation and for persons in need of God's healing touch.

SESSION FIVE

SPIRITUAL PRACTICE

Read John 1:1-5, 9 prayerfully. Take time to breathe deeply experiencing God's calming presence. As you breathe deeply, visualize a healing light entering your body, filling your body, mind, and spirit from head to toe. After a few minutes, visualize this healing light surrounding and protecting you. Conclude by giving thanks for God's healing light, illuminating all things.

QUESTIONS

1) How do you understand the nature of "sin" in the first century? In what ways was Levi considered a "sinner"? What are the consequences of being considered a "sinner"? How might Levi have experienced his sinful social status?

2) What occupations might be considered "unclean" in today's culture? Are there persons we treat differently as a result of their occupation or social standing?

3) How do you understand the statement: "the place God calls you to is the place where your deep gladness and the world's deep hunger meet"? How do you understand vocation or call? How do people develop a sense of calling and vocation?

4) Where have you experienced people leaving their professions to seek what they consider a "higher good"?

5) How do you understand Paul's comment in Philippians: "The good work God has begun in your life God will bring to fulfillment ... and it will be a harvest of righteousness." What good work do you imagine God doing in your congregation? What harvest of righteousness do you see emerging in your life and in your congregation?

6) In what ways can your congregation help people discover their vocation or purpose in life?

CONCLUDING PRAYER

As a group, take a moment to lift up the many gifts you experience in your congregation or your group. Take a moment to share your own gifts in the church. Give thanks for the abundance of God's gifts in your life and congregation.

SESSION SIX

SPIRITUAL PRACTICE

Begin this session with the practice of "centering prayer."

Centering prayer is practiced by:

» Begin with a prayer
» In the silence, focus on a particular prayer word, such as "peace," "joy," "love," "Shalom," "light," and "love."
» If your mind wanders, bring it back to the prayer word without judgment.
» Take ten minutes for centering prayer.

QUESTIONS

1) Where do you see "isms" today – sexism, racism, ageism – in today's world? What are the consequences of these "isms" today?
2) How do you understand Jesus' encounter with the Syrophoenician woman?
3) How do you understand Jesus' opening message from Luke 4:18-19 – "the Spirit of Lord is upon me ..."? Is Jesus' message meant solely for individuals or for the larger political and social context?
4) Who are our "others"? Who are the people that we consider outsiders in our community, in our church, and in other nations? How do we bridge the gap between ourselves and others?
5) What do you think of the concept of "healing at a distance"? Do you think prayer shapes the health conditions of others? Do you think prayer enables God to do new things?

6) What role does intercessory prayer play in your life? Have you experienced any answers to prayer? How do you deal with disappointment in terms of unanswered prayer?

7) What negative comments do you hear these days? How should we respond to negativity? In what ways can we respond to the culture and political wars?

CONCLUDING PRAYER

Conclude with the practice of centering prayer.

SESSION SEVEN

SPIRITUAL PRACTICE

Begin with the practice of *lectio divina*, focusing on Mark 8:22-26. Share your insights with one another and the large group.

QUESTIONS

1) What experiences have you had with healing services – in your church or elsewhere? What are your responses to television healers? How do you evaluate their healing services?

2) What does it mean to be described as God's healing partner? Do you think your prayers and actions make any difference to God?

3) Have you had experience with dramatic healings? Have you had experience with gradual healings?

4) Using your imagination, why do you think that Jesus was unable to heal the sight impaired man fully in his first try?

5) What is your response to Mark 6:5-6: "And he could do no deed of power there, except he laid his hands on a few sick people and cured them. And he was amazed at their unbelief." Do you think we limit God's power by our actions? Do you think our actions influence God's impact on our lives and the world? If we make a difference to God, how might this shape our ethics, spirituality, and prayer lives?

6) How do you evaluate the new age comment "you create your own reality"? In what ways is this similar to the comment made by some Christians that "we can name it [what we need] and claim it [as a reality]"?

7) Where have you heard people "blame the victim" for her or his condition? In what ways might this be unfair and harmful?

CONCLUDING PRAYER

Conclude by sharing events in the past week where you experienced God's presence. Take time to give thanks for God's gentle presence in your life and the world.

SESSION EIGHT

SPIRITUAL PRACTICE

Begin with a *lectio divina* practice, focusing on Mark 5:1-20. Let God's insights speak in and through you. Share your insights with your neighbor and the large group.

QUESTIONS

1) What is your initial response to the idea of "demon possession"? Do you think that such experiences are possible? Or are they a result of psychological disorders? Or can both explanations for illness be plausible?

2) What stands out in the encounter of Jesus and the "demon possessed" man? What is the attitude of Jesus toward the demons? How do the demons respond to Jesus?

3) Do you believe that political upheavals can be the source of physical and mental illness? Where have you seen social situations shaping a community's or person's well-being?

4) Why do you think Jesus sent the demons into the swine? Is this a political as well as religious statement?

5) What do you think of the idea that groups of people can be controlled by unhealthy "powers and principalities"? Where have you observed group minds doing evil things? Where have you observed groups doing good things?

6) Does it make any difference to use different names – mental illness terms – instead of terms related to demon possession?

7) How can your congregation best respond to persons with severe mental health issues? How can your congregation best understand persons who have been harmed by traumatic experiences, whether in war or family life?

8) Consider the following questions raised in the text: If God is omnipresent, is there a movement toward health subtly present

even within mental health disorders? Does the God who seeks abundant life for all creation move subtly through our neuroses and disorders of body, mind, and spirit luring them, perhaps even against their will, toward wholeness? Can demonic spirits, if such exist, also hear the gospel and experience redemption?

9) Where do communities resist healing of vulnerable people? Why might healing be hazardous to the status quo?

CONCLUDING PRAYER

The Celtic Christian tradition has a body prayer described as the "caim" or "encircling." In this prayer, you rotate in a circle, with your index finger pointing outward, creating a place of safety and protection. Often an invocation such as "nothing can separate me from the love of God" or "Christ above, below, in front, and behind me," is used as you encircle yourself in God's blessing.

SESSION NINE

SPIRITUAL PRACTICE

Begin today's practice by taking what my friend and fellow author describes as a "beauty break." After convening the class with a prayer, invite the class to take five minutes to walk around the church or outside, noticing objects of beauty. Share your experiences of beauty with one another.

QUESTIONS

1) How do you understand the nature of "blessing"? Where have you experienced blessings?

2) What do you think of the author's discussion of blessing various encounters and situations?

3) Contrast the realities of blessing and cursing. Where do you experience "cursing" personally, relationally, and politically? What is the impact of cursing in our social context?

4) Larry Dossey speaks of medical hexing and prayer mugging, and notes that 5% of the population pray that negative things happen to others. What do you think of praying for other peoples' harm? Is this really a prayer? Are limitations that physicians put on our health outcomes "hexing" their patients? How do we balance realism with hope in dealing with illness?

5) How would it feel to hear God say to you, "you are my beloved child in whom I am well pleased"? How might it change your life if you accepted God's blessing?

6) What was the place of children in the first century? What problems do children face today?

7) What words of blessing might Jesus have said to the children? What words of blessing can the church say to children? Where do children need a blessing today? In what ways can we as a community bless the children?

CONCLUDING PRAYER

Conclude in a circle, inviting each person to enter the center of the circle. As the group lays hands on the person, have someone say, "You are my beloved child, in whom I am well pleased."

SESSION TEN

SPIRITUAL PRACTICE

Begin today by practicing breath prayer, breathing deeply God's healing and calming spirit. Open to God with each breath.

QUESTIONS

1) Where are the greatest sources of stress for people today? What is the impact of stress on your emotional and physical life?

2) How do understand the following description of the disciples: *For many were coming and going, and they had no leisure even to eat.* In what ways is this comment characteristic of your life? Where do you feel burdened and busy these days?

3) Do you have a special place for your spiritual practices – a holy or thin place? Where is this special place? (According to Celtic Christian spirituality, a "thin" place is a spot where God and the world meet. It is a sacred place where we can more fully experience God's presence.)

4) How do you understand the relationship between action and contemplation? In what ways do we need action to be healthy? In what ways do we need contemplation to be healthy?

5) Do you ever take a Sabbath? What would it be like to take a day-long break from the internet or some other habitual behavior? What are the benefits of Sabbath-keeping?

6) In what ways can congregations encourage good health among their members? What could your congregation do to help members reduce stress?

7) What do you think of the reality of "compassion fatigue"? In what ways can we nurture compassion over the long haul?

8) Which are you more like – Mary or Martha? Which of the health practices discussed at the end of the chapter are most challenging for you? Which would be most helpful to you?

CONCLUDING PRAYER

Conclude with a time of centering prayer as described in Chapter Ten's "Healing Marks" or described in the session guide for Chapter Six.

SESSION ELEVEN

SPIRITUAL PRACTICE

Begin with the meditation on God's healing light, described on Session Five (p. 165).

QUESTIONS

1) Take a moment to read Mark 9:18-21. What is your initial response to this passage?

2) What is your attitude toward Christians using complementary/alternative medicine? Is complementary/alternative medicine ever discussed in your church? How would your congregation be different if complementary medicine were integrate into its worship and practices?

3) Early Christian theologians noted, "wherever truth is present God is its source." How do you understand this statement? How does it influence your attitude toward other religions and medical practices?

4) How do you think religion and medicine should interact? How do you evaluate theological positions that maintain using medicine is contrary to Christian faith?

5) What is your response to the Roman Catholic Bishops' critique of reiki healing touch? Do you think complementary medical techniques should be taught in church?

6) How can Christians influence the practice of Western medicine? What do you think of physicians who pray with their patients? Would you like your physicians or nurses to pray with you?

7) How do you respond to the author's "Guidelines for Christians" section (p. 141)? What are the dangers, if any, of Christians using complementary/alternative medicine?

CONCLUDING PRAYER

Conclude the gathering with the ancient practice of anointing with oil. One by one invite people to enter the healing circle. If they wish, let each person have the opportunity to anoint and be anointed, using an extemporaneous prayer, or a prayer such as "In the name of Jesus Christ, I anoint you, that you might experience the fullness of God's healing power to transform you and those for whom you pray."

SESSION TWELVE

SPIRITUAL PRACTICE

Begin with a prayer of thanksgiving for the twelve weeks you've met together and God's presence in your life. Then, practice *lectio divina*, focusing on Mark 16:1-8. Share with your neighbor and the large group.

QUESTIONS

1) Read Mark 16:1-8 and then, after a pause, Mark 16:9-20. What is most interesting or inspiring about the short version? What do verses 9-20 add to the resurrection accounts?

2) Put yourself in the place of the women coming to the tomb. How do you think they felt as they came to the tomb? How do you think they felt as they discovered the tomb was empty?

3) The gospel gives an interesting description of the women's response to the "angelic" message and commission to tell the disciples: *So they went out and fled from the tomb, for terror and amazement had seized them; and they said nothing to anyone, for they were afraid.* How do you think you would have responded?

4) Read the encounter of Jesus and Mary Magdalene, described in Luke 20:11-18. What spiritual lessons does it contain? In what ways is it inspiring?

5) What is your image of everlasting life? What is the relationship between what we do in this time and our eternal destiny?

6) What is the "sting" of death, described in I Corinthians 15? What are your greatest fears regarding death and dying – your own and your loved ones? In what ways does faith in Christ's resurrection enable us to respond creatively to the reality of death?

7) Why is it important for the gospel writers to describe the Risen Jesus as having wounds? In what ways is a suffering Christ essential to our healing?

8) What is the most important thing that you've learned in this series? What is the most important spiritual lesson you have experienced over the past several weeks?

CONCLUDING PRAYER

Begin your final prayer with a time of breath prayer. Visualize healing light entering your whole being with every breath. Now visualize your breath surrounding you, protecting and empowering you, and sending healing light into the world. Experience this healing light expanding in wider and wider circles, impacting, filling your room, the church building, your community, nation, and the planet, and then out into the wider universe. Then, experience this light contracting again ... from the wider universe to the planet, nation, community, church building, your room, and yourself. Conclude by giving thanks for God's healing light giving life and light to all things.

SELECTED TEXTS

MARK'S GOSPEL/JESUS

Brian Blount and Gary Charles, *Preaching Mark in Two Voices*. Louisville: Westminster./John Knox, 2002.

Marcus Borg and N.T. Wright, *The Meaning of Jesus: Two Visions*. San Francisco: Harper One, 2007.

John Dominic Crossan, *The Historical Jesus: The Life of a Mediterranean Jewish Peasant*. San Francisco: Harper One, 1993.

John Dominic Crossan, *Jesus: A Revolutionary Biography*. San Francisco: Harper One, 2009.

Daniel Harrington, *What are They Saying About Mark?* New York: Paulist, 2008.

Richard Jensen, *Preaching Mark's Gospel: A Narrative Approach*. Lima, OH: CSS Publishing, 1996.

Joel Marcus, *Mark 1-8: A New Translation with Introduction and Commentary*. New York: Anchor, 2000.

John Meier. *A Marginal Jew*, Volume 2. New York: Doubleday, 1993.

William Placher, *Mark*. Louisville: Westminster/John Knox, 2010.

Gerd Theissen, *The Miracle Stories of the Early Christian Tradition*. Minneapolis: Fortress, 1983.

Bonnie Thurston, *Preaching Mark*. Minneapolis: Fortress, 2002.

Bonnie Thurston, *The Spiritual Landscape of Mark*. Collegeville, MN: Liturgical Press, 2008.

Mary Ann Tolbert. *Sowing the Gospel*. Minneapolis: Fortress, 1999.

Ben Witherington. *Mark: The Gospel of Mark: A Socio-Rhetorical Commentary*. Grand Rapids: William Erdmanns, 2001.

N.T. Wright. *Simply Jesus: A New Vision of Who He Was, What He Did, and Why It Matters.* San Francisco: Harper One, 2011.

HEALING AND WHOLENESS

Herbert Benson, Larry Dosssey, John Polkinghorne, et al. *Healing through Prayer: Practitioners Tell Their Story.* Toronto: Anglican Book Center, 1999.

Herbert Benson, *Timeless Healing: The Power and Biology of Belief.* New York: Scibner, 1997.

Larry Dossey, *Be Careful What You Pray For.* San Francisco: Harper One, 1998.

Larry Dossey, *Healing Beyond the Body.* Boulder, CO: Shambala, 2003.

Larry Dossey, *Healing Words.* San Francisco: Harper One, 1995.

Larry Dossey, *Prayer is Good Medicine.* San Francisco, Harper One, 1997.

Larry Dossey. *Space, Time, and Medicine.* Boulder, CO, 1987.

Bruce Epperly, *God's Touch: Faith, Wholeness, and the Healing Miracles of Jesus.* Louisville: Westminster/John Knox, 2002.

Bruce Epperly, *Healing Worship: Purpose and Practice.* Cleveland: Pilgrim Press, 2006.

Abigail Evans, *Healing Liturgies for the Seasons of Life.* Louisville: Westminster/John Knox, 2008.

Craig Keener. *Miracles: The Credibility of the New Testament Accounts,* Two Volumes. Grand Rapids: Baker Books, 2011.

Morton Kelsey, *Healing and Christianity.* Minneapolis: Fortress, 1995.

Harold Koenig, *Is Religion Good for Your Health? The Effects of Religion on Physical and Mental Health.* New York: Haworth, 1997.

Harold Koenig, *The Healing Power of Faith.* New York: Simon and Schuster, 2001.

Jeff Levin, *God, Faith, and Healing: Exploring the Spirituality-Healing Connection.* San Francisco: Wiley Books, 2002.

David Levy, *Gray Matter*. Carol Streams, IL: Tyndall House, 2011.

Bruce Lipton, *The Biology of Belief: Unleashing the Power of Consciousness, Matter, and Miracles*. Los Angeles: Hay House, 2011.

Dale Matthews, *The Faith Factor: The Proof of the Healing Power of Prayer*. New York: Penguin, 1999.

Candace Pert. *The Molecules of Emotion: The Science Behind Mind-Body Medicine*. New York: Simon Schuster, 1999.

Tilda Norberg and Robert Webber, *Stretch Out Your Hand: Exploring Healing Prayer*. Nashville: Upper Room, 1998.

Cash Peters, *A Little Book About Healing: The Transformative Healing Power of Faith, Love, and Surrender*. Beverly Hills: Penners, 2011.

Agnes Sanford, *The Healing Light*. Minnneapolis: Macalester Park Press, 1972.

Flora Wuellner, *Miracles: When Christ Touches Our Deepest Needs*. Nashville: Upper Room, 2008.

Flora Wuellner, *Prayer, Stress, and Our Wounds*. Nashville: Upper Room, 1986.

ALSO FROM ENERGION PUBLICATIONS

Introducing participatory study guides to theology and doctrine

... a helpful corrective and foundation for a subject that has become untethered from the Bible, theology, and reality.

Rev. Dr. Geoffrey D. Lentz
First United Methodist Church
Pensacola, Florida

ALSO BY THE AUTHOR

... a solid presentation of the historical, sociological, and ideological issues that arise from reading Phillippians.

Lisa Davison
Professor of Hebrew Bible
Phillips Theological Seminary

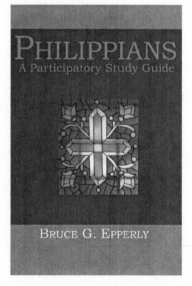

MORE FROM ENERGION PUBLICATIONS

Personal Study

Finding My Way in Christianity	Herold Weiss	$16.99
Holy Smoke! Unholy Fire	Bob McKibben	$14.99
The Jesus Paradigm	David Alan Black	$17.99
When People Speak for God	Henry Neufeld	$17.99
The Sacred Journey	Chris Surber	$11.99

Christian Living

Faith in the Public Square	Robert D. Cornwall	$16.99
Grief: Finding the Candle of Light	Jody Neufeld	$8.99
Crossing the Street	Robert LaRochelle	$16.99

Bible Study

Learning and Living Scripture	Lentz/Neufeld	$12.99
From Inspiration to Understanding	Edward W. H. Vick	$24.99
Luke: A Participatory Study Guide	Geoffrey Lentz	$8.99
Philippians: A Participatory Study Guide	Bruce Epperly	$9.99
Ephesians: A Participatory Study Guide	Robert D. Cornwall	$9.99

Theology

Creation in Scripture	Herold Weiss	$12.99
Creation: the Christian Doctrine	Edward W. H. Vick	$12.99
The Politics of Witness	Allan R. Bevere	$9.99
Ultimate Allegiance	Robert D. Cornwall	$9.99
History and Christian Faith	Edward W. H. Vick	$9.99
The Church Under the Cross	William Powell Tuck	$11.99
The Journey to the Undiscovered Country	William Powell Tuck	$9.99
Eschatology: A Participatory Study Guide	Edward W. H. Vick	$9.99

Ministry

Clergy Table Talk	Kent Ira Groff	$9.99
Out of This World	Darren McClellan	$24.99

Generous Quantity Discounts Available
Dealer Inquiries Welcome
Energion Publications — P.O. Box 841
Gonzalez, FL_ 32560
Website: http://energionpubs.com
Phone: (850) 525-3916

CPSIA information can be obtained at www.ICGtesting.com
Printed in the USA
BVOW041145100213

312869BV00005B/329/P